MOTHER DEAREST

WENSLEY CLARKSON

BLAKE

Published by Blake Publishing Ltd,
3 Bramber Court, 2 Bramber Road,
London W14 9PB, England

www.blake.co.uk

First published in hardback in 2005

ISBN 1 85782 552 7

British Library Cataloguing-in-Publication Data:

A catalogue record for this book is available from the British Library.

Design by www.envydesign.co.uk

Printed in Great Britain by Creative Print and Design

1 3 5 7 9 10 8 6 4 2

Papers used by Blake Publishing are natural, recyclable products made from
wood grown in sustainable forests. The manufacturing processes conform to
the environmental regulations of the country of origin.

Every attempt has been made to contact the relevant copyright-holders, but
some were unobtainable. We would be grateful if the appropriate people
could contact us.

To Terry,
The ultimate survivor

'PLEASE! PLEASE LET ME OUT OF HERE!'

The screams and moans coming from that hallway closet had became like audible wallpaper in the Knorr household. No one acknowledged the sounds, but then Theresa Knorr had insisted on stuffing towels underneath the door to the closet so that it muffled her daughter's cries for help. No one seemed concerned about Sheila, except Terry, by now fourteen years of age.

She strained her ears to listen for any tell-tale signs of her sister's condition inside that small closet. A few days after she was locked in there for the second time, Terry heard Sheila rustling around, desperately peeling off her clothes because of the sweltering eighty-five degree heat that overwhelmed the day and much of the night.

Sheila would never leave that closet again …

INTRODUCTION

It would be reassuring to believe that murder was a gross abnormality, a dramatic departure from respected ethical standards that restrain civilised man from sur-rendering to his basic instincts. Once, murder was con-sidered to be beyond the pale, irreconcilable with the rest of mankind. But now, advances made in our knowledge of ethnology, evolution, and human psychology present challenges to such banal assumptions which cannot be ignored. Unfortunately, as man has become more civilized, intelligent, creative, and dominant, he has also become more murderous.

Statistically, murder is still rare in proportion to the population. So the type of crimes committed by Theresa Jimmie Knorr are even more baffling, as they fall into three categories: domestic, episodic, but seemingly random (although this later turned out not to be the case).

Murder is a purposeful deed which often makes the killer despicable to the rest of us, but perversely renders him healthy and admirable in his or her own eyes.

Criminologist Brian Masters studied in great depth the motivation of many notorious killers, and he concluded: 'It is hardly surprising that the murderer is reluctant to show remorse for his (or her) acts. It would be a retrograde step, a kind of psychological suicide ...'

As an author and former crime reporter, I have written about many of the most notorious criminals of modern times, from the appalling killings committed by Charles Manson and his flock of disciples to the ultimate crime of passion that made American serial killer Aileen Wuornos one of the most infamous murderesses of modern times.

However, I can never forget my response as a parent when I first became aware of the murders committed by the mother featured in this book. How could a mother kill her own flesh and blood? Even worse, how could a woman break that special bond which is supposed to exist between mother and daughter?

But then mother love can take many forms: hatred, derision, sympathy, inspiration, devotion, self-sacrifice, companionship; destruction, jealousy, admiration, affec-tion, desolation, and, it now seems, even murder.

Mother love is supposed to mean love of a mother for her

children. It is a two-way process, which means that the child gradually rises until she is in the ascendent – the succourer, not the succoured. Your mother is your mother for always. Your one and only mother. Your mother for all time. You cannot divorce your mother, and if you happen to be her daughter, you are the same sex as her, out of the same mould. It is like a series of those Russian wooden dolls, the sort that fit inside each other, painted with different floral dresses, but shaped the same and becoming smaller and smaller.

Men may still rule the genealogical tree, but it is the female side of the family that has a truer inheritance. When a woman has a baby, it is her mother, not her father, she turns to, and if that baby is a girl, in due time she will turn to her mother. That is a real family tree. The family tree of women.

It may be significant that the mother described in this book lost her own mother at a young age. She had no one to turn to at the start of parenthood. No one to guide her. No one to tell her how to cope.

As I began to investigate the circumstances behind the crimes featured in this book, I uncovered such a vast catalogue of hidden abuse that I could not help asking the same question over and over again: Why? The blatant violence committed in the name of the family cannot all have been thoughtless. What hidden factors contributed to this tragedy? Why did authorities ignore the pleas for help by one sister and force her back into that house of horrors and in effect sentence her to death? Why did so many not believe the only surviving daughter when she told authorities what had happened inside that household?

I take no specific stance in presenting the facts in this book as they have been revealed to me through painstaking research and extraordinary access to tape-recorded statements made to investigators during the course of their inquiries, as well as dozens of interviews. I have simply recalled events as they were told by everyone involved.

But, if ever a case needed to be read about, then this is it. The very fabric of the modern day family unit is already under enough severe pressure. The story of the Knorrs is a warning of just how bad things can get and why all of us, as responsible adults, have a duty to our children to do something to arrest the decline before it is too late.

It is hardly as if the warnings have not been made in the past. For years, so-called experts have been telling us about childhood abuse and its terrifying aftermath.

The battered child syndrome has been described as unrecognised trauma by radiologists, orthopedists, paediatricians, and social workers. It is a significant cause of childhood disability and death.

Unfortunately, it is frequently not recognised, or, if diagnosed, is inadequately handled by physicians because of hesitation in bringing cases to the proper authorities.

Yet, incredibly, not so long ago in Western society, unbridled parental domination was an enduring tradi-tion whose roots can be traced to the Old Testament.

Later generations took this biblical command quite

literally. Under the Old English common law, children were regarded as the property of their fathers. Parents could require their children to work for them, or place them in indentured servitude in return for payment. Absolute obedience was not an issue, for children who attempted to rebel were whipped and beaten or placed in workhouses.

The harsh treatment of children went hand in hand with prevailing moral and religious beliefs that 'childhood was an inherently evil state.' This tradition carried over to American shores where, in 1646 in the Massachusetts Bay Colony, newly arrived citizens (ironically, escaping oppression) enacted the Massachusetts Stubborn Child Law. Parents who claimed that their children were 'stubborn and rebellious' and 'disobedient of voice' – could seek one of several 'state reprimands' including execution. Obviously, democracy and due process were not things the Pilgrims wanted in their homes.

Children universally attach themselves to their carers. This is a survival mechanism necessary to provide the needs that a child is unable to satisfy alone. Certainty of the presence of a safe base allows for normal emotional and cognitive development ... In the absence of such a safe base, as in cases of child abuse and neglect, a child goes through a variety of psychological manoeuvers to preserve maximum protection. Abused and neglected children often become fearfully and hungrily attached to their carers, with timid obedience and an apparent preoccupation with the anticipation and avoidance of abandonment.

In his book, Soul Murder, Albert Shengold went so far as to say that what he described as soul murder was 'the deliberate attempt to eradicate or compromise the separate identity of another person. The victims of soul murder remain in large part possessed by another, their souls in bondage to someone else ... Torture and deprivation under conditions of complete dependency have elicited a terrible and terrifying combination of helplessness and rage – unbearable feelings that must be suppressed for the victim to survive.'

When a child is punished severely and unfairly, it becomes a mind-splitting or mind-fragmenting operation because many children have to keep in some compart-ment of their minds the delusion of good parents and the delusive promise that all terror, pain, and hate will be transformed into love.

PROLOGUE

In the early 1990s, one of the most appalling examples of multiple child abuse ever seen was uncovered thanks to the dogged efforts of one young woman who narrowly escaped with her life after witnessing a catalogue of terror inside her own family home.

It had all begun almost ten years earlier in a desolate area of forest near the High Sierra Mountains, in central California. It is a bleak expanse of rugged terrain – the perfect dumping ground for a thousand secrets. A place where a bear or a mountain lion is more likely to come across human remains than a deputy sheriff or a forest ranger. Nobody knows how many bodies are out there. It is pure luck if anyone stumbles upon them.

And, even when human remains are discovered, chances

are that those murderers will never be arrested. Most bodies are not even identified. The cops who patrol the area call them body dumps, and over the years they've included every type of death: decapitations, burned-out cars, strangulation, emasculation, impaling; a few had been injected with battery acid, and then there are the ones who've simply been tossed down ravines.

Even when these tragic victims are found, they all too often end up being buried in an unmarked grave with just the words 'Jane Doe' on a tiny headstone. Unclaimed, unloved, a waste of a life ...

Truck driver Robert Eden did not hesitate to stop when he was flagged down by housewife Maybel Harrison on the northbound section of Highway 89, just half a mile north of Squaw Valley Creek, on the edge of those same High Sierras, near Tahoe City, in Placer County, California. It was dawn on 17 July 1984:

'There's a brushfire by the creek,' explained Maybel breathlessly.

Eden grabbed the chemical fire extinguisher from the cab of his truck and ran to the blaze just thirty yards from the side of the road. Minutes later he also doused the still burning fire with a three-gallon can of water, just to be absolutely certain it was completely out. Then he found himself transfixed by what Maybel Harrison thought was a mannequin-the toes sticking out from under the cinders confirmed it.

'That's a body ...'

The silver duct tape used to gag the victim and tie her wrists was still visible on the charred remains.

Just over an hour later, with emergency services surrounding the scene, Tahoe City Fire Department Captain Ron Collins, a member of the Arson Task Force – began examining the rubble with a hydrocarbon detector, which determines the presence of flammable liquids in fires. It took less than a minute to establish that the fire had been started deliberately.

Tahoe City Detective Russell Potts then carefully collected three soil samples starting at a point four feet north of the corpse. Then he crouched down to collect more soil just six inches from the charred remains before removing one last sample from a different angle to the body. They were all carefully packaged in contamination-free cans, sealed and put aside for eventual analysis by the Department of Justice.

By 7.50 a.m. detectives had already informed the Department of Justice that they were dealing with a homicide and requested that a photographer and crimi-nologist get to the site immediately.

At 10:05 a.m. Placer County Sheriff Donald J. Nunes arrived with a police photographer. Within the hour, criminologist Michael Saggs from the Department of Justice and four officials were snapping away furiously with their cameras at the grotesquely twisted body that consisted of a charred left arm propped up on her elbow, with the hand straight up in a curled position. The lower portion of the left leg was detached at the femur and was lying on the ground approximately three inches away from the end of the femur. The right arm was at the corpse's side and the right leg extended straight from the body at a weird right angle.

Investigators did not allow Mark Dafforn from the discreetly named 'county removal service' to take control of the body until 2:00 p.m. Detectives frequently find homicide scenes have been tampered with before they even arrive at a location but, on this occasion, they actually had the luxury of more than eight hours of light to minutely examine the area for clues. Police sifted through a vast array of belongings found near or on the body, including perfume, writing paper, necklaces, bracelets, clothing, a toothbrush, even a fork and soup spoon. But there was no actual evidence of the victim's identity.

Detectives decided it was time to rechristen the charred remains as Jane Doe #4873/84.

That day, an urgent telecommunication was faxed to the US Missing Persons Bureau.

It read:

WEA 18–22 YRS. BLN HAIR, SLENDER BUILD, POSS WEARING A YELLOW NYLON HOODED PARKA AND UNKNOWN COLOR CORDUROY PANTS.

THIS DEPARTMENT IS CURRENTLY INVESTIGATING A HOMICIDE WHICH HAS OCCURRED IN OUR COUNTY AT APPROXIMATELY 0545 HRS THIS DATE. VICTIM WAS FOUND BY A PASSING MOTORIST.

VICTIM HAD SILVER DUCT TAPE COVERING HER MOUTH, AND AROUND BOTH WRISTS. VICTIM WAS THEN SET ON FIRE AT THE SIDE OF THE ROAD. VICTIM WAS VERY BADLY BURNED, AND UNRECOGNISABLE. VICTIM HAD SOME PERSONAL PROPERTY WITH HER, POSS IN 2 PLASTIC GARBAGE BAGS. BAGS CONTAINED MISC PERSONAL PROPERTY, INCLUDING CHILDRENS CLOTHING, HOWEVER BAGS WERE ALSO BURNED.

REQUEST YOU CHECK YOUR RECORDS FOR ANY MISSING PERSONS WHICH MAY MATCH THIS JANE DOE, OR ANY SIMILAR HOMICIDES.

THANKS IN ADVANCE.

REFER: LT CADER/DET LIDDLE CASE #4858-84 PLACER COUNTY SHERIFF'S SUBSTATION, DRAWER 171, TAHOE CITY, CA. 95730 DONALD P. NUNES SHERIFF/CORONER (916) 583-1561 7/17/84

1358 HRS NTS/PJO

The day after the discovery of the corpse, detectives sent the victim's fingers off to Sacramento to have prints taken off them after police began to suspect that the body might have been that of a missing woman called Georgia Darlene Taylor. The practice of removing fingers from a corpse is a little-known procedure, which is rarely referred to because it is considered by some to be a disrespectful way to treat the dead. But investigators across the world have been using this method of checking fingerprints for years, because it saves having to move entire corpses across state lines and in some cases international borders. One time, a Florida medical examiner was transporting a victim's fingers across the state when he was stopped by the Florida Highway Patrol for allegedly speeding. When the official explained to the motorbike cop what he had in the box on the seat next to him, the officer refused to believe him and forced him to open the container. The policeman fainted on the spot.

Back in Sacramento, an examination of the prints on the duct tape found wrapped around part of the body confirmed that two men implicated in the Georgia Darlene Taylor case were not involved in the death of this particular Jane Doe. To add to their frustration, investigators could find no match for the prints on the state computer file.

The subsequent autopsy – performed by forensic scientist Dr A. V. Cunha at the DeWitt Centre Morgue on 23 July – provided the police with few clues to Jane Doe's killer. All they could be certain of was that she was five feet three inches, weighed approximately 115 to 130 pounds, and had blond hair and blue eyes. However, the examination did uncover that she had died after being bound, gagged and set on fire. Dr Cunha also found a large ovarian tumour in the corpse, which indicated she had been severely beaten in the stomach.

Dr Cunha was also puzzled by the apparent presence of

two recent wounds in the right back and lower buttocks region. But the corpse was too badly charred for him to ascertain the exact cause of each injury.

However, the one aspect of the discovery of the body that had investigators very concerned were the nappies found near the body, plus what they thought were children's clothing. Detectives feared that this Jane Doe might have been with a child who could have been killed elsewhere. Only later did they acknowledge that the 'children's clothing' were actually just skimpy teenagers' blouses.

The final pathological diagnoses by Dr. Cunha referred to *ninety per cent* burns to the body and described those previously inflicted wounds as being of 'uncertain significance.'

Dental examiner James Nordstrom was able to be more helpful. He reported that the victim had a chipped tooth, possibly caused during an attack, and a number of fillings that might make identification easier.

However, a computer check could not match up those dental records, and Placer County detectives believed it was unlikely they would establish the identity of the corpse, let alone solve the case. Putting a name and family to a murder victim is usually the most significant development in trying to investigate a homicide. Without a name, there is basically no one to interview, unless of course there were some witnesses.

So it was that, just eight days later, Sheriff Donald Nunes made a formal request to have the body of their Jane Doe #4873/84 frozen at the Sacramento County Coroner's Office until further enquiries could be made. Publicly, police were continuing their investigation as energetically as ever. Privately, they were winding down the inquiry because they had reached a complete and utter dead end. By freezing her body in case it should be needed for evidence/identity purposes at a later date, the sheriff was simply going through the motions just in case a miracle occurred and they got a break on the case.

Jane Doe's face was even reconstructed by police artist Jim Hahn on the day before her remains were taken off to be frozen in Sacramento. Detectives hoped that the drawing might provoke some response once they printed up posters, but they did not hold out much hope.

On 1 August 1984, Placer County investigators tried one last telecommunication message, this time to narcotics units, vice units, biker units, intelligence units and sex-crime units nationwide in a final effort to identify their Jane Doe. They got no response.

At the end of August a continuation report filed by Placer County Sheriff's Department was sent to Sheriff Nunes informing him that more than two hundred possible leads had been investigated into the identity of the corpse. The report concluded that their biggest hope was that, when schools reopened in the later part of September, they might get a reaction to those posters distributed to every school district in the state.

When autumn came and that drew another complete blank, the Sheriff's Department – rather than incur any more expensive freezer charges at the Sacramento Medical Examiner's Office – released the body for burial at the New Auburn District Cemetery in Auburn. The funeral was unattended. No one ever knew her real name.

The following spring, the FBI contacted the Placer County Sheriff's Department in Auburn, with 235 possible matches for the Jane Doe. But they all proved negative.

The main problem for police was that unsolved murders in the rural Sierra counties divided by major highways were a logistical nightmare. Virtually all the homicides were imported; in other words, they happened elsewhere and then became their case because the bodies were dumped on their turf.

Most cases tended to be shifted quietly to the back of homicide files. Detectives prepared to wait for a lead that, in most cases, never surfaced. The mystery of Jane Doe #4873/84 would remain unsolved for almost ten years.

Almost one year later, on 21 June 1985, a fisherman discovered a corpse in a box on the edge of Martis Creek Lake, located just east of Highway 267 in the densely forested Martis Valley area of Nevada County, California, just fifteen miles from where that other body had been dumped and set on fire. The fisherman immediately alerted Elmer Barber, camp host at the Martis Creek Lake Campground, to the existence of the corpse. Barber went straight to the local sheriff's office where he told Deputy Gary Costley all about the 'body in the box.'

At 12.40 p.m. Officer Costley drove up the paved road, past the Tahoe Truckee Sanitation Agency building, turned east and then followed the road as it swept to the north and headed on to another paved road clearly marked with a campground sign. Just past the campground, the road turned to gravel and dirt before sweeping to the left and straightening out once more at the location by the lake where Elmer Barber said the body had been found. Deputy Costley found the box – measuring just twenty-five inches by nineteen inches – in amongst a clump of young weeping willows, which covered an area of only about twelve feet by eight feet near the water's edge.

Costley tentatively pulled open the top of the box – clearly marked 'Popcorn Cups' – to examine the contents. Inside were stained sheets, blankets and plastic bags. On closer inspection, Costley could clearly see a left arm and shoulder, the left side of a torso and the left hips of a human body in a foetal position. The body ranged in colour from a light, almost white colour, to green, purple, and black. There was also a cloth ligature around the deceased's neck and wrist.

Tyre tracks near the scene were evident, but because of rain that morning they were not clear enough to be identified.

At 2.00 p.m. six more policemen arrived on the scene followed by Deputy D.A. Tom Eckhardt. The officials had another problem on their hands besides the homicide: whose jurisdiction covered the crime scene – Placer or Nevada County? On the basis of the corpse being discovered a few feet inside their county line, Nevada took on the investigation.

By the time the body was removed a few hours later by Medical Examiner's official Joe Aguera and taken to the Tahoe-Truckee Mortuary for an autopsy the next day, police had combed the area but failed to find any other clues apart from the box. Its grotesque contents also included a discarded pair of white panties and a pair of dirty white socks. Investigators noted that the Jane Doe had three pierced right ears and two pierced left.

The Nevada County Coroner's Record form filled in that day contained few actual facts, just more than a dozen 'unknowns' written in the information boxes. The coroner had been unable to determine whether the victim had starved or suffocated in that box. Another Jane Doe was about to be christened after death.

It would take almost ten years before the tragic lives of those two seemingly unconnected corpses would be linked to reveal the horrific story that you are about to read.

ONE

'Hell hath no fury like a woman scorned ...'

Theresa Jimmie Sanders's facial structure might not have been particularly classic, and the perpetual frown she wore gave her blue eyes more of a haunted look than the clear-eyed confidence that she wished they'd had, but eighteen-year-old Theresa was still brunette and pretty, if not beautiful. Her complexion was clear and smooth, and her five-foot-five-inch frame was lithe and bosomy.

Resident Sheriff's Deputy Fred May had vaguely noticed Theresa a few weeks earlier when she and her husband moved into one of the row of small, single-storey houses just near the railroad tracks about fifty yards down from his own home on Elm Avenue in Galt, a township twelve miles south of Sacramento, California. He therefore instantly recognised the striking-looking teenage mother when she turned up on his doorstep at 9.15 a.m. on 6 July 1964.

'You gotta come quick. I shot my husband in the arm.'

Within a few minutes, Galt Police Chief Walter Froehlich was also on the scene and the two men accompanied the young girl – with her baby in her arms – to her home at 586 Elm, where they found her husband Clifford lying facedown in the doorway of the kitchen. His only wound appeared at first to be in the wrist. But the .30-30 calibre slug had travelled through his body and embedded itself in his heart. He was dead.

The two officers immediately glanced at an old-model deer rifle leaning against a wall in the front room. Noticing their interest, Theresa told the chief, 'I grabbed the gun to make him keep from hittin' me and it went off.'

She told them a tearful story about how her husband had begun to thrash her with the butt end of the rifle and how, miraculously, she had been able to wrestle the weapon away from him. She even said to the policemen that Clifford Sanders had been arrested just two weeks earlier for assault and battery, but she had decided not to press charges.

'Her reaction was mild, I'd say,' recalled Froehlich more than thirty years later. 'But different people react in different ways.'

Theresa Sanders was booked and taken to the Sacramemo County Jail. Her baby son Howard – still ten days off celebrating his first birthday – was taken by the sheriff to one of Theresa's relatives north of Sacramento.

The day after the shooting, the *Sacramento Bee* daily newspaper ran a dramatic photo of pretty, petite Theresa Sanders being led into the county jail by stern-looking Galt Police Matron Mary Templeton, a whole head and shoulders taller than her prisoner. Arms folded, her hair cut in a fashionable bob style, Theresa Sanders looked as if butter would not melt in her mouth.

The headline that accompanied the photo exclaimed: murder charge is due in galt death

Its first attention-grabbing paragraph read:

Deputy District Attorney Donald Dorfman said he planned to file a murder charge today against eighteen-year-old Mrs. Theresa Sanders of Galt in the deer rifle slaying of her husband. Clifford Sanders, 23, was slain yesterday morning in the couple's small Galt home. Investigators reported the .30-30 bullet apparently grazed off his left wrist and lodged in his heart …

The shooting was the talk of Galt – a sleepy railroad town split in two by the old Highway 99 that runs up from Stockton and Modesto to Sacramento. The Sanders had moved to their tiny, one-bedroom house from Sacramento earlier that summer. Conditions inside the house were especially cramped because of the presence of Theresa's father, James Cross. There was no actual bath or shower in the $75-a-month property, and baby Howard was usually bathed by Theresa in the kitchen sink. The difficult conditions were not helped by the roar of endless cargo trains regularly thundering along the railroad, just a few yards from their front door.

The red-roofed, white building they lived in was really no bigger than a single garage, and contrasted drastically with the larger, more luxurious three- and four-bedroom homes on Elm, just fifty yards in the opposite direction to the railroad tracks. Up until the shooting, Theresa, Clifford and Howard slept in a small room at the back of the house, while her father James slept on a couch in the living room, just by the rickety front door.

After her arrest, Theresa Sanders told Deputy District Attorney Donald Dorfman that her husband had threatened to beat her on the morning of the shooting and that he was packing to leave her. But she also admitted that he had not actually beaten her since the incident that almost led to him being arrested two weeks earlier.

It then transpired that, just minutes before the killing, Theresa Sanders went into the bedroom where the rifle was kept loaded, got the gun and returned to the living room as her husband was about to open the door, apparently to leave home for good.

'I remember holding the gun and having my finger on the trigger, but then everything went blank,' she told investigators at the time.

Theresa Sanders's invalid father, James Cross, informed detectives that the gun was kept loaded with the safety catch on. Significantly, he also added that it would have been necessary for her to deliberately cock the hammer before firing it.

The couple had been estranged at the time, but Clifford Sanders – a carpenter for the American Safeway Scaffolding Company – had moved back into the Galt home with his wife and father-in-law about three weeks before the shooting.

The only witness to the killing was the couple's eleven-month-old baby, Howard. He said later he was haunted by the knowledge that he was there when his mother shot his father dead, even though he was too young to actually remember the killing.

Within a few hours of Theresa Sanders's arrest for murder, she told investigators she was pregnant with another child by her late husband. That unborn child was Sheila, a girl whose future was to be irretrievably connected to that fatal shooting.

On 4 August 1964, Theresa Sanders entered a plea of innocent by reason of self-defence in a Sacramento court to the charge of murdering her husband. She insisted she only intended to scare Clifford Sanders when the rifle she was holding went off, sending that bullet into his heart.

Her performance at the trial was considered very emotive by lawyers and police alike. She even tearfully told her own lawyer, 'All I want to do is to go home and take care of my baby.'

Deputy District Attorney Donald Dorfman was not so convinced. He argued for a first-degree murder conviction and insisted that Theresa Sanders was jealous of her husband's attentions to other women and had regularly threatened to kill him.

'Not every murderer looks like the witch in *Snow White*,' he told the jury.

Theresa Sanders looked a lot less like the witch than she did Snow White: pure, sensible, sweet.

Dorfman insisted that, just after the shooting, Theresa Sanders ran across the street and told a neighbour she had just shot her husband. Then, her cheeks burning and her pretty face twisted into a scowl, she added, 'No man's gonna leave me.'

When Dorfman tried to introduce that evidence in court, the judge ruled it as inadmissible because the neighbour was the wife of the deputy sheriff and Theresa should have been advised of her rights.

Two extra bailiffs were even assigned to the trial after Theresa's husband's brother, Tommy Sanders, said he was 'going to get a gun and shoot someone'. A witness at the trial, Tommy openly displayed his anger towards Theresa.

At one stage, the judge even permitted Theresa Sanders's attorney, Robert A. Zarick, to carry a loaded handgun to court.

Once, he took the gun out of his briefcase, turned to the victim's family, seated in the courtroom, and said, 'None of you maniacs are going to get me like Cliff tried to get her.' It was a trial filled with controversy.

Theresa Sanders's pitiful story of life at the hands of a wife beater who also frequently boasted of his prowess with other women was totally contradicted by her husband's sister Mrs

Lydia Hansen. She told the court that her brother worked hard, never drank and gave his wife all his earnings. These claims have a familiar ring to them, as Theresa's children later complained bitterly about how their mother made them hand over all their earnings every week.

Hansen, Theresa's sister-in-law at the time, also insisted that her brother never once threatened or hit his pretty young wife. In fact, Hansen recalled that Theresa always drove her husband to work and back to be sure no other women ever got to look at him. She also kept his clothes in rags for the same reason, and gave Clifford Sanders just fifty cents for lunch money so he could not go to a restaurant where another woman might get a look at him.

Hansen also revealed that Theresa Sanders had shot at her husband once before, and that her brother had shown her the bullet hole in the floor.

'I believe with all my heart that Theresa Sanders planned to kill my brother,' she insisted to the hushed courtroom.

But then, in a remarkable show of compassion, Hansen said she wanted Sanders to go free so she could raise her brother's children. Hansen's final statement may have helped more than anything else to sway the jury, and that decision could well have contributed towards the tragedies that later occurred in Theresa's household.

On September 10 – just twelve days after the trial began – a jury of nine men and three women told Judge Charles W. Johnson that they found Theresa Sanders not guilty as charged, after deliberating for an hour and forty-five minutes.

Theresa, dressed in a baby-blue maternity dress on that last day in court, wept when the verdict was announced. Then she approached the jury box. Many of the jurors smiled at her. She was desperately trying to thank them; but the tears just would not stop streaming down her face.

One female juror grinned warmly at Theresa Sanders and got up to put her arm around the innocent young mother. It was a touching scene.

Theresa Sanders held her weak little chin high and pursed her thin lips together in triumph.

Former police chief Froehlich always believed that District Attorney Dorfman thought he had a clear-cut case against her. Dorfman had tried to give the court the impression that Theresa Sanders was a cold, calculating killer. A few days later – in yet another strange twist – Theresa coolly walked into Dorfman's office to reclaim the rifle she had used to kill her husband.

She even told Dorfman, 'I liked the way you came after me.'

Theresa Sanders was oddly in awe of the young prosecutor, and years later she even tried to hire him to handle the divorce proceedings for her third marriage. She also recommended Dorfman to that same tragic child, Howard, when his own marriage began to crumble more than twenty years later. Theresa told her family that Dorfman was a superb attorney and she had great respect for him.

But Chief Froehlich's most vivid memory of the aftermath following Theresa Sanders's arrest was that of little Howard Sanders. Froehlich personally drove the child to a suburb north of Sacramento to stay with relatives while Theresa was in custody.

'That poor little fella. I always wondered what happened to him.'

Thirty years later, Howard Sanders has just one reminder of his father still in his possession. It is a rusted handgun with a broken handle.

Theresa Sanders could not stand the thought of moving back into the house where she shot her husband dead, so she, her father and her baby Howard moved to the district of Rio Linda, North Sacramento, after her acquittal on murder charges. It was familiar territory for Theresa, since she had been born in Rio Linda on 14 March 1946.

Little is known about her true upbringing, apart from the fact that her mother died in her arms when Theresa was about twelve. Her father had a close bond with his daughter and remained a part of her life right up until his death in 1985. But Theresa Sanders spun such a vast web of lies to so many different people that much of what she told about her past now has to be completely discounted.

She told some friends about pleasant countryside, life on a farm and riding horses every day. But, to others, she reshaped her past to include an unhappy childhood, poverty-line existence and a daily regime of brutality at the hands of a series of stepmothers. The truth is that no one really knows much about Theresa's life before she was arrested for murdering Clifford Sanders in July 1964.

By Christmas of that year, Theresa Sanders had put her

brush with the law behind her. Already in the later stages of her second pregnancy, she went back to calling herself by her maiden name, Theresa Cross, and settled back into life in a modest two-bedroom house at 6608 Cherry Lane, Rio Linda.

At twenty-two minutes past midnight on 13 March 1965 – the day before her own birthday – Theresa, still just eighteen, gave birth to Sheila Gay Sanders, at the Roseville District Hospital, just a few miles from her home. On Sheila's birth certificate Theresa had written *Deceased* under the sections marked 'Husband's Present or Last Occupation' and 'Kind of Industry or Business'.

By the end of the following year, Theresa revived her interest in men and met handsome young marine Robert Wallace Knorr. She had also moved to a comfortable house on Tioga Street, in San Francisco. Life seemed to be looking up.

Theresa gave birth to her third child, Suesan Marline Knorr, at 1.50 a.m. on 27 September 1966, at the USAF Hospital on Mather Air Force Base, in central California. The birth certainly caused a stir among Robert Knorr's family back in Minnesota. After all, he was only eighteen and the mother of his child was just twenty – and they had not even bothered to get married.

However, Knorr family pressure eventually resulted in Robert and Theresa going through a wedding ceremony in 1966. On 15 September 1967, a son, William Robert, was born. On 31 December the following year came Robert

Wallace Jr. Theresa Knorr was just twenty-two years old and the mother of five young children.

According to Theresa's son, Howard, Robert Knorr's temper, combined with his later experiences in Vietnam, soon turned him into a highly volatile character. The children came to fear his presence in the house. One time, Howard had to pick his baby brother Billy Bob off the floor when Knorr Sr. kicked him all the way across the room into a toilet and his head split open.

Theresa Knorr all too frequently became the last line of defence against her ill-tempered husband.

By the time a sixth child, Theresa (Terry), was born on 5 August 1970, at the Sutter Memorial Hospital, Theresa Knorr had already separated from her husband Robert. At the end of September that year, their divorce was finalised.

Two marriages followed in fast succession for Theresa Knorr. First there was Ronald Pulliam. Of all her husbands, he seems to be the only one who no one has a bad thing to say about. The children even called him 'Dad' when they all lived together in a comfortable house on Morris Avenue, in Sacramento.

Pulliam later said he just wanted to forget he had ever had a relationship with Theresa Knorr, let alone a marriage. 'I don't want to talk about her. It all happened a long time ago,' were the only words he would utter. Pulliam and Theresa broke up in the early seventies. A man called Bill Bullington then came on the scene, but none of the surviving children ever knew if their mother actually married him.

11

By 1973 the family had moved into their one and only large house in Orangevale, West Sacramento. It was to be their home for longer than all their other places put together, and actually had enough space for the entire clan. Theresa then met and married a wealthy newspaper executive called Chester Harris, who worked on the now defunct *Sacramento Union*.

Around this time, Theresa Knorr began putting on weight. She also started to grow her long dark hair further down her back, giving her the appearance of some kind of medieval witch. Chet Harris had an interest in the occult, and he seemed to have found a keen disciple in Theresa.

TWO

'Abusive parents thrive on isolation and a
perverted sense of privacy.'

PAUL MONES, *WHEN A CHILD KILLS*

There is no evidence of the much stressed, overworked Theresa Knorr hitting out impatiently at her children when they were toddlers. She actually seemed to enjoy bringing up the youngsters in those early years. She saw herself as the all-powerful mum who'd ensure her children's survival through thick and thin.

Theresa Knorr often took youngest daughter, Terry, and her brother Robert to the local Dairy Queen for a slap-up lunch followed by a big dollop of ice cream, and made them both promise not to tell their older brothers and sisters, who were at school, and would no doubt be jealous that they had not been taken out for a treat.

Theresa Knorr also made many other sacrifices on

behalf of the children. One time, she even pawned her favourite diamond bracelet so that she could buy Terry some school clothes.

She was the only person the children knew as consistently loving them and taking care of them. She was their life. Their saviour.

Throughout this period, Robert Knorr Sr. was like a black cloud looming over the Knorr household. He still came to visit his four children just about whenever he felt like it, and sometimes ended up kicking the hell out of the kids if the mood suited him. His temper got even more frayed when he suffered a serious shrapnel wound in the stomach in Vietnam. He also walked with a slight limp.

Theresa Knorr's weight was still rising rapidly and she had taken up reading the Bible at every opportunity. She would sit in the living room and recite from the Bible, often underlining quotations and sometimes even forcing the children to join in as well.

But in another corner of that large house in Orangevale, a much more disturbing incident was occurring. Terry, just six years old, was being molested by her brother Howard, who was thirteen at the time. It was an awful introduction to an even more awful life within those four brutal walls.

Years later, Terry told investigators, 'I didn't know what he was doing; well, I knew what he was doing wasn't right, but I wasn't, you know, I was afraid to tell anybody, and ... I went to my mum because it hurt.'

Theresa Knorr was outraged when she heard that Howard

had molested his half sister. She broke a chair over the boy's back and seriously beat him to make sure he never did it again.

Howard Sanders later confessed to having illicit sex with his sister in dramatic tones to two stunned Placer County investigators during a tape-recorded interview conducted at his home in Sacramento on 16 November 1993.

POLICE OFFICER: I'm going to make this very short and sweet. There's been allegations of molestation and that you molested Theresa, your sister. Are those allegations true?

SANDERS: Yes.

POLICE OFFICER: And that was sodomy, anal sex.

SANDERS: Yes.

Terry will never know if that attack by her brother sparked the eventual terrors that filled the Knorr household, but, shortly after being molested by Howard, bad things started to happen.

The first incident occurred when the mother of one of Terry's best friends, Jennifer – who lived on Sutton, just around the corner from the house in Orangevale – called at Theresa Knorr's front door to offer her some of her daughter's clothes as a gift.

Theresa Knorr was furious. She thought Terry was going around telling people that the family didn't have any money, that they were so poor they couldn't afford to buy the children clothes.

15

Once Jennifer's mother had gone, as later recounted by Terry, Theresa Knorr grabbed her youngest daughter and made her strip naked before dragging her through the house.

Then she grabbed a piece of rope, wrapped it around Terry's neck and threw it over a door. Theresa Knorr's two sons, Billy Bob and Robert, then held the rope, forcing Terry to stay in one position while her mother beat her with a weeping willow limb until she almost passed out. Terry remained jammed against the door throughout.

Theresa Knorr's violent outbursts seemed to be fuelled by her introduction to witchcraft by Chester Harris following their marriage.

Theresa later began claiming that her daughter Suesan was involved in devil worshipping. She even made veiled references to Suesan plotting to kill her mother before she reached the age of eighteen. *'To fulfil her contract with the devil ...'*

According to Terry, something happened between Chester Harris and Suesan. It was something which drove a wedge between her and her mother. It also influenced the break-up of Theresa Knorr's marriage to Harris.

After the split with Harris, Theresa Knorr began frequently disappearing from the house on Bellingham, in Orangevale, for days at a time, leaving Howard – just fourteen –to look after the rest of the clan.

On one occasion she took off for at least four days after running out of the door of the house in front of the children. She returned with the police, claiming that Howard had threatened her. Howard – sitting in the living room with a friend – immediately burst into tears because he was so upset by his mother's abandonment and her false accusations against him.

Years later Howard wondered whether Theresa Knorr had been suffering from a nervous breakdown at the time. What other reason could there be for a mother to run out the front door and leave her children in the care of a fourteen-year-old?

Theresa Knorr gave her son a bizarre explanation when he asked where she had been during those four days she disappeared.

'She told me she had found some pennies and she threw these pennies away and that, you know, these pennies showed back up in the motel where she was staying, and no matter what she did, these pennies kept showing back up, you know,' said Howard.

'I mean, I didn't understand it at the time. But looking back on it, I mean, obviously they were paranoid delusions. And that goes along with somebody that's having a nervous breakdown.'

Sometime after this, Theresa Knorr stopped getting out of bed and getting dressed. She never took a shower, and refused to go outside for weeks at a time. But she still managed to wield the hand of discipline if required.

Theresa Knorr stopped punishing her son Howard when he was a strapping fourteen-year-old – six feet and 190 pounds – and highly likely to retaliate against his overweight, overbearing mum. The last time he was beaten by her, she wielded her favourite weapon – a two-by-four with the words 'Board of Education' written across it.* He cannot remember the reasons for the punishment, but the words exchanged between mother and son provide a cold insight into their relationship.

After his mother's final painful smack on his backside with the two-by-four, Howard turned around to her and said, 'You done now?'

'Yup. I guess you're too big to whip any more.'

Howard's worst legacy from those beatings was his vicious temper. Not surprisingly, life at that house really screwed him up. 'I had a real problem with my anger, you know, real problem with my anger. That's what led me into a bad marriage, and I ended up going to jail for it and that wasn't the first time I ever got in trouble about violence. So, yeah, it screwed me up pretty good. I had a lot of demons to work out,' he told investigators years later.

But, while Theresa Knorr might have decided not to beat her eldest son any more, there was no such reprieve for her daughters.

She was convinced they were going to go out and be promiscuous. She wanted to keep control of the girls so they

* Henry Lee Lucas, one of the most notorious serial killers of modern times, was beaten regularly by his mother with a two-by-four at his home in Blacksburg, Virginia. He went on to receive eleven murder convictions, including a death penalty, six life sentences, two seventy-five-year sentences, and one sixty-year sentence.

would never be involved with boys. That meant clamping down on them – not even letting them go out and socialise with other teenagers.

Theresa also passed on the mantle of responsibility to her boys, especially Howard at that time, because he was the eldest. It put the teenager under immense pressure. He was already working part-time as a cook at a local restaurant called Joe and Dotty's, on Auburn Boulevard, to help the family survive. He had learned how to cook by preparing meals for his brothers and sisters. But now he was going to have to be the father as well. The other children accepted Howard as a father figure for the period he remained at home. He was respected, even feared. Basically, he took the place of a husband. That also meant frequently being the disciplinarian of the family.

There were numerous occasions when Theresa Knorr would let Howard do her spanking for her with that familiar piece of two-by-four. She was proud of having trained him in the art of inflicting punishment.

Sometimes Howard would make the children hold their ankles as he smashed the board on their bottoms or would lay them on the floor before spanking them.

These spankings were such vicious beatings that none of the children ever forgot them.

Bruises were commonplace, especially when Howard used that two-by-four piece of wood, the so-called 'Board of Education'.

Theresa Knorr still got involved in the really serious

punishments. On many occasions the children being punished would end up with bruises all over their bodies. Theresa even introduced a switch-style riding crop to inflict extra pain on her flock of children. When she used the switch, the injuries were so serious that the other children would dab peroxide on the cuts all over the back of whoever had been punished. As he was the oldest and the biggest, no one dared argue with Howard. He even devised rules and regulations that the other children had to obey, or face dire consequences.

Howard's career as main male enforcer in the Knorr household continued until he retired, at sixteen, after starting to work full-time as a chef. Howard was the sort of guy who, if the front door was slammed, went around to the back door;and, if the back door was locked, he tried the windows; and, if the windows were barred, he would haul out a sledgehammer.

But working outside the home began to give him a new perspective on life.

'I was seeing more of life and started to realise that these weren't right, you know, that beating kids wasn't right,' he says.

As well as questioning his mother's orders, Howard actually began standing up against Theresa Knorr on behalf of his other brothers and sisters. The punisher was transforming into the protector.

Theresa was no longer physically strong enough to stand up against Howard, but she had no intention of stopping the punishments being inflicted. She just tried to make sure he wasn't around when she handed out her own special brand of discipline.

Howard never actually hit his mother, but he did come close to it frequently. One time he grabbed her and threw her against a wall. Then he smashed the wall right next to her head with his fist and put a hole in it. The children used to snigger every time they walked past the dent in the plaster.

But it was sisters Suesan and Sheila who got the brunt of their mother's vicious temper. Howard and Terry both remember one day when Theresa Knorr pulled Sheila's canine tooth out with her bare hands because it was not growing straight.

At school, Sheila's big ears earned her the nickname Dumbo. Life was extra tough on her. Physical abuse at home and verbal taunting at school. Was there no escape?

Theresa Knorr's drinking also became excessive at this time and she'd frequently pack all six children in the family station wagon and leave them in the car outside bars in Orangevale. Visits to drive-in movies were just as distressing for the youngsters.

'She'd end up getting bombed. Then she'd pass out and we'd have to wait for her to wake up to go home,' recalled Howard.

For many of their childhood years the kids veered from malnourishment to being force-fed vast quantities of fatty food. Sometimes teachers would take pity on some of the Knorr children and provide them with sandwiches and the occasional hot meal. But it is tragically clear the diet inside that household had serious effects. By the time he was twelve, Howard's diet included a daily consumption of alcohol and drugs, packs of cigarettes and the occasional slice of bread smothered in peanut butter, jam or cheese. These years of inconsistent, damaging diet, especially during child-hood, may well have resulted in stunted development of some of the Knorr children. It also created levels of stress and fear that no ordinary family should ever have to suffer. But there was much worse to come ...

THREE

'If my mother loved you, she loved you greatly. But if you were on the outs with my mother, she would make you feel like you were all alone in the universe, that nobody cared about you and you weren't worth anything. So you always wanted to be on the good side of my mother.'

HOWARD SANDERS

That's odd, neighbour Sean Martin remembered thinking as he walked out into the backyard of his house opposite the Knorr family home in Orangevale, the dog is not moving.

Bijou lay deathly still as twelve-year-old Sean tried desperately to wake him up. He pulled and tugged at the animal, but there were no signs of life in his tiny body.

A few minutes later Sean and his big brother Chris flashed a light down the dog's throat: they just could not accept that their pet – part cocker spaniel, part poodle – was dead. When it dawned on them what had actually happened, both boys started sobbing.

Life on Bellingham Way had been littered with odd incidents ever since the Knorrs moved in nine years earlier. Those who visited the house likened it to an out-of-control runaway train ride consisting of drug taking, excessive alcohol and repeated violence towards one or other of the Knorr children. The family got a reputation in the area, which meant they were blamed for just about every strange occurrence on the street. To make matters worse, Howard Sanders – now in his mid-teens – was hanging out with all the wrong types.

Neighbour Sean Martin grew up with the entire Knorr family from the mid-seventies up until when Theresa Knorr sold the house in 1982. He witnessed dozens of odd incidents, but the death of his dog Bijou is a typical example of how rumours could quickly spread about the 'weird' Knorr family.

It all began when Bijou nipped Theresa's youngest daughter Terry on her leg when she was teasing him in the front yard of Sean's home. Terry – eleven at the time – was not that bothered about the injury, but Theresa Knorr was convinced the dog had rabies, and she reported Sean and his family to the SPCA and got the dog quarantined for a month.

Bijou was actually released from quarantine after only four days because he was given a complete clean bill of health. The next day Sean walked into the backyard and found the animal dead.

No one knows who killed the dog, but Sean believes it was poisoned. The incident went down in Bellingham folklore as gossip flew around that Theresa Knorr had killed the dog. But no one ever proved if the story was true.

The Knorr house in Orangevale had a strangely designed interior. The orange and white drapes were thumbtacked to the wall, and there were just bare lightbulbs – no lamp shades.

The furnishing inside the house consisted of a very basic leaf table with six chairs around it. There was one tatty couch. But there were no knick-knacks or posters or pictures on the walls, and the TV was on constantly. The carpet was a dreadful, sickly, pea-green colour. It seemed as if personal touches were non-existent inside the Knorr family home.

Sean Martin – now in his thirties – got into trouble with Robert one time when they were both just twelve years old. The two boys stole hundreds of dimes out of a neighbour's house.

After being caught, the boys accused each other of committing the evil deed: Sean's mother marched him down to her neighbour's house to apologize for stealing. Then she took him to the Knorrs.

On their arrival at the house, the front door opened and there was a stench of marijuana wafting on to the porch. One of the Knorr children hollered for their mother, but was ordered to slam the door shut, and Sean's mother never did actually get to talk to Theresa Knorr about their respective sons' illicit behaviour.

Sean frequently heard screaming and pounding on the walls while playing on the sidewalk near the house. But, instead of reporting the noises, he just tried to avoid going near the house. Other neighbours commented on the noises, but they also did nothing.

On other occasions, Sean heard streams of profanities

coming from Theresa Knorr inside the house. It surprised him that an avid Bible reader should use such foul language.

Sean only ever got to talk to Theresa Knorr during her rare trips out to the local store when she would walk past his front yard. The conversation was always brief and ineffectual. Theresa Knorr – whose weight had soared beyond the 200-pound mark by this time – would waddle up the street with her long dark hair down to her waist and wearing a vast pair of bell-bottom pants. She looked like a huge, fat version of the lady out of the Addams Family, he remembered years later.

Sean also suspected some sort of devil worshipping going on inside the Knorr house. It coincided with the time the children were made to shave their heads by their mother and wear certain types of clothes. But, once again, no one did anything to bring the family to the attention of the authorities.

Not surprisingly, the Knorr children never wanted to go home when they were out playing with their friends. Terry and Billy Bob were constantly around Sean's home, which had become known locally as the 'Kool-Aid house' because it was such a relaxed place. The Knorr children stayed there for meals and told their friends they rarely got a proper meal at home. Other neighbours also felt sorry for them and would feed them regularly.

Older sister Sheila was frequently dispatched by Theresa Knorr to pick up the children from neighbours' homes. She was always very well-mannered and would turn up at the door and say: 'OK kids, time to come home.'

Sean was in the same class at school as Robert for four years, but during that time the youngster was often absent. Robert also surprised his friend Sean by regularly referring to his mother in a detrimental fashion.

'He said she was off her rocker. That she was a hermit with emotional problems. He just kept saying she was crazy,' recalled Sean.

One time, Theresa Knorr set fire to the backyard of the house on Bellingham for no apparent reason. When Sean rushed over to see if he could help, he had to go through the garage to the back yard, and noticed hundreds of articles of clothing just ripped to shreds, lining the concrete floor. The fire destroyed the back fence, but Sean never forgot the sight of all those clothes. No one ever did find out why the fire occurred.

All the Knorr children – except for Howard Sanders – were very skinny and undernourished-looking at this time. Sean also noticed welts on Robert's back from where his mum had beaten him with a belt.

Sean and Robert regularly did drugs together. Sometimes they would sneak out and smoke pot in the nearby park. Later, they did some more serious stuff together.

Some mornings, big brother Howard drove the rest of the kids to school in Theresa Knorr's Ford LTD. Sean would often go along for the ride. The children were always much friendlier in the car, out of reach of their mother.

None of the sisters dated anyone on the street, as they were kept in the house because Theresa Knorr did not want them to get promiscuous. She also refused to give her daughters an allowance.

Sean – whose best friends in the family were Robert and Terry – never tried to date any of the Knorr girls, but his brother Chris was very keen on Sheila for a while, although she did not feel the same way about him. Chris and Sheila even went on a field trip with the school one time, but the relationship never got going.

Sean's family, taking pity on the Knorr children, used to hold birthday parties for them at their house because Theresa Knorr would not allow their friends inside her home.

Inevitably, all the unhappiness inside the Knorr household resulted in Suesan running away from home on a regular basis. The neighbours always knew when she was on her way because there would be a loud commotion outside the house as Suesan ran down the garden path to a waiting gas guzzler filled with her biker-type friends, who would screech off down the street once she'd climbed in.

One time, a bunch of her friends turned up in a station wagon with a Starsky and Hutch-type stripe down the side. They grabbed Suesan, pushed her in the car and took off at high speed. At first neighbours thought she'd been kidnapped, but it later emerged that Suesan had happily gone with them because she could not stand life inside the Knorr house.

Once, Suesan ran away with a practising satanist whom the rest of the family believe introduced Suesan to the occult – and that that contributed to her mother's hatred towards her. But a lot of this information was supplied by Theresa Knorr to her children, tempered with exaggerations and lies to ensure that the other brothers and sisters stayed on their mother's side. There were other recurring problems within the family, like Howard Sanders sexually abusing his half-sister Suesan just to get back at his mother. It is not hard to imagine how much influence this had on the dysfunctional situation inside the Knorr household.

Then there was the time all six children were in the backyard of the house on Bellingham, weeding the ground with just a teaspoon each. Howard and his siblings were ordered by Theresa Knorr to completely clear the yard of thistles and weeds and not to go anywhere for four days until they had pulled every one of them out.

The children soaked the ground of the backyard with water before going down on their hands and knees with their spoons. Howard was strong enough to pull the weeds out with his hands, but the others spent hours digging up tiny plots of earth as Theresa Knorr watched from the back window to make sure no one was being lazy.

Not surprisingly, most of the family's neighbours on Bellingham steered clear of the Knorrs, apart from a woman named Cherise Frederick.

Theresa Knorr seemed to have a real friend in Cherise, who was one of the few people ever to be allowed inside the house and actually made to feel relatively welcome.

But Theresa Knorr's real motives in befriending Cherise seemed to be centred around her knowledge of the Bible and religion, and they would spend hours talking about their favourite quotations.

The last couple of years at the house on Bellingham mainly featured a running battle between Suesan and her mother. Suesan was having a lot of emotional problems – besides regularly fleeing the house with her oddball friends, she was not helped by the fact that her mother kept ranting on about her daughter's 'contract with the devil'.

Whenever Suesan acted strangely, Theresa Knorr would tell the other children that Suesan was 'up to her usual crap again.' She had little or no sympathy for her deeply disturbed daughter.

Howard tried to stay away from the house on Bellingham because he could not deal with what was going on. But his mother just would not stop going on about Suesan playing with witchcraft and being a devil worshipper. Howard kept telling his mother that Suesan simply had mental problems. That she needed a doctor. But Theresa Knorr knew best.

At one point, Suesan, then just fifteen, ran away and was arrested by police. She told them about some of the punishments inflicted by her mother, and they took her to the Child Protective Service offices in Sacramento, where she pleaded to be made a ward of court. The CPS even visited the house on Bellingham in response to allegations of parental abuse made by Suesan about her mother.

A number of meetings at the CPS offices followed. But officials did not believe the teenager's story, and her mother was allowed to regain custody of her daughter. Theresa

Knorr convinced them that Suesan was just an uncontrollable child, and she assured the CPS she could cope with her. Youngest daughter Terry was forced to lie to CPS officials who visited the house, after being threatened with a beating by her mother. Years later, when police tried to find out the names of the social workers who recommended that Suesan be allowed back home, they were told that all the records had been purged under a five-year rule.

Even the other Knorr children were astonished when Suesan was returned home, since they presumed she would never be allowed to move back into the house on Bellingham.

After Suesan was compelled to move back, it became painfully obvious to Terry that Theresa Knorr was going to punish the teenager even more than before her escape. Her two other daughters were also scared and couldn't understand why their mother hated all of them so much.

One day, after years of never being seen, Robert Knorr Sr. visited the house in a bid to see his four children. Theresa Knorr sent Howard's girlfriend Connie – who was living with Howard at the time – out to talk to Robert Sr. because she knew that he did not know her. Connie had to pretend she was the new owner of the house and that Theresa Knorr and her family had moved on months earlier. Theresa Knorr wanted to prevent Robert Sr. from ever seeing his children again.

During those last few months that the family lived at Bellingham, Howard Sanders was heavily into dealing drugs. He later claimed Theresa Knorr knew all about the illicit activities and even helped run the narcotics business in his absence. And, when Howard did not have enough cash, he paid his mother the rent in drugs, which she either smoked or made him sell during subsequent drug deals.

One time, Howard was even tipped off by a friend at the Sheriff's Department about a planned raid on the house by private detectives, and cleaned it out of drugs hours before they arrived.

Howard's vast array of drugs turned the house into a virtual pharmacy. Howard was known locally as the mushroom man. He had acid. He had connections for coke, crack and he always had two different types of weed on him. He also had connections with someone who ripped off pharmacies for speed. He often got the drugs in their sealed bottles straight out of the stores.

With the influx of drug trade to the house came the occasional brush with a number of unsavoury characters, who accused Howard Sanders of ripping them off during drug deals.

On one occasion, the Knorr family were warned by some Hell's Angels who lived around the corner that they were going to come over and 'rape all the women'. The Angels were angry that Howard had taken away some of their business. Howard even gave his girlfriend Connie that old .22 of his dad's to carry for protection whenever she went to the local store.

Theresa Knorr also frequently issued warnings to Connie, but they had nothing to do with the drug trade. She was concerned about Connie's safety, living under the same roof as her daughter Suesan.

Theresa Knorr told Connie to always lock her bedroom door at night because, she explained coolly, 'Suesan is going to try and kill you because she does not like you at all.'

Connie was terrified by the threat of murder, especially since she suspected it was partly caused by Suesan's jealousy because Howard had committed incest with her.

But there was another reason why Suesan disliked Connie so much. When she and Connie had been at Pershing Junior High together in Orangevale, Connie and her brother had frequently teased Suesan by calling her 'fishface' because she wore big, thick glasses and looked like a nerd.

Suesan Knorr greatly contributed to her reputation as the devil's child within the family by cutting off her mother's eyelashes, removing bits of her long, spindly fingernails, and stealing a few strands of her waist-length black hair during a daring midnight raid on her mother's dingy bedroom. Theresa Knorr claimed afterwards that she did not wake up during the incident because Suesan had drugged her coffee with masses of sleeping tablets.

Theresa Knorr was furious when the children refused to tell their mother who was responsible. She systematically burned each of them with cigarette butts until they told her who had done the evil deed.

Theresa Knorr knew it was probably Suesan because she suspected that the specimens had been removed for some sort of witchcraft ceremony. She also believed Suesan was jealous of her good looks.

Once Theresa Knorr had confirmed that it was Suesan, it marked the start of a series of horrendous attacks. Theresa Knorr utterly detested her daughter's daring behaviour, and she began claiming that Suesan was suffering from sexually transmitted diseases as well. Shortly afterwards, Theresa Knorr told Howard's girlfriend Connie, 'She is a witch, and the only way you can kill a witch is by burning them.'

Theresa Knorr warned Connie that, any time she cleaned her hairbrush or trimmed her nails, she should flush it all down the toilet because Suesan could get the remnants and use them for her devil worshipping. Theresa Knorr also told Connie that Suesan would be after her blood eventually.

Even Howard Sanders – hardly a saint by anyone's reckoning – continued to try to get Suesan some discreet medical attention, because he firmly believed she had a mental problem. One day he went over to Connie's stepdad's place on Pershing, in Orangevale, and asked him for advice on how to get his sister committed. But Theresa Knorr once again ignored Howard's pleas when he voiced his concern, and she banned him from ever mentioning the subject again.

The beatings rapidly escalated after the eyelashes incident. Howard Sanders walked in on his mother whipping Suesan with a plastic tube one day. He immediately snatched it from his mother and broke the tube into tiny pieces. But much of the damage had already been done.

Suesan, five feet five inches tall, was approximately the same height as her mother, but Theresa Knorr vastly outweighed her. She had turned into a turtlelike waddler who rocked from side to side as she moved. Her face had become almost square from overeating. Her expressions, even during the most violent exchanges, ran the gamut from stolid to grave.

Sometimes the violence inflicted on Suesan would subside long enough so that Theresa Knorr could sit her bruised and battered daughter down and make her read excerpts from the Bible. Theresa Knorr also talked about calling in priests to perform exorcisms to get the devil out from within her daughter.

Around this time, Theresa Knorr's drinking increased. She would often keep the children up all night, interrogating them on the different oddities of the Bible.

Theresa Knorr indicated her true feelings about her daughters by always referring to them as 'your sisters' during any conversations with the boys. She would spit the words out.

Her possessiveness also knew no boundaries. She tried to encourage her children not to attend school because she wanted to keep an eye on the girls and get the boys out to work from as early an age as possible.

Suesan's last school was Arcade High School, on Watt Avenue, but she only got as far as seventh grade when her mother pulled her out of school, just as she'd do with Terry a few years later. Sheila managed ninth grade at Casa Robla before she stopped attending.

About the only one who continued with his studies was Billy Bob. By all accounts he had a good head on his shoulders. He was smart and good at sports. The other children believe he stayed in school so much because he was trying to keep out of his mother's reach. *Amazingly, despite all the children's appalling record of absence from school, no one investigated the family's home life to find out where the problems lay.*

Both Robert and Billy Bob had part-time jobs before they turned fifteen, and Billy Bob was extremely bitter about his mother having put all the utilities in his name so that he had to pay for everything out of his modest pay packet. Billy Bob saw it as yet more evidence that his mother was trying to control his life.

It also had a chillingly familiar ring to it. For Theresa Knorr had made every man – including the husband she shot dead – part with his wages the moment he walked through the door.

FOUR

'All happy families resemble one another; every unhappy family is unhappy in its own way.'

TOLSTOY, *ANNA KARENINA*

Theresa Knorr rocked back and forth in her chair, Terry later recalled. Back and forth. Back and forth. Not a glint of emotion in her steely blue eyes. Just an empty stare at the person sitting just a few feet away.

In front of her – crumpled at the kitchen table like a rag doll incapable, afraid, to defy any order – was her seventeen-year-old daughter Suesan, whose sin was to be prettier and thinner than her mother and who was rumoured to be mixing with the devil. It infuriated Theresa Jimmie Knorr to even look at Suesan. She accelerated the pace of her movements on that red rocking chair. Her eyes locked on Suesan. All the children knew that was a sign.

The chair creaked under the weight of her 250-pound frame.

Theresa Knorr pushed a pot filled with macaroni cheese into her hands.

It was the first of four boxes of the stuff that she would make her daughter consume that night.

Suesan shook as she grabbed the saucepan filled to the brim with food. The scorching hot pot sizzled as it touched the skin of her bare legs.

Suesan's first few mouthfuls brought little response from her mother.

'Don't get that on the floor.' Theresa Knorr spat the words out with disgusted contempt.

Suddenly the door to the kitchen burst open and stick-figured, blond Terry rushed in. She stopped dead in her tracks when she saw that her mother was administering her daily dose of punishment to one of her five brothers and sisters.

'Oh! I, uh ... I didn't mean ...'

Twelve years old, Terry Knorr looked from her sister Suesan to her mother, then slowly turned her gaze back to her sister with a look of recognition that verged on apathy. Her pallid face seemed to shrink.

'Oh,' she repeated dully, taking an involuntary step backwards.

It was yet another cruel and twisted moment from within the four battered walls of the Knorr household, but it would remain etched in Terry's memory for the rest of her troubled life.

A few weeks later – in June 1983 – Theresa Knorr decided to give her two younger sons – Robert, fourteen, and Billy

Bob, fifteen – some lessons in the art of corporal discipline.

Terry recalls that Robert stood behind Suesan at the end of the hall of that comfortable detached home in Orangevale and held her arms back while his brother Billy Bob put on sinister-looking slim black leather bicycle gloves almost like a surgeon preparing for an operation. Theresa Knorr told her son that the gloves were essential for ensuring that no one could detect evidence of the beating Suesan was about to receive.

Theresa Knorr was apparently unhappy because her daughter had not gained enough weight in the previous few weeks. No female in that house was going to look prettier and younger than her. And all that devil talk was ringing in her ears.

Then Theresa crashed her own clenched fist deep into her daughter's stomach. The teenager flinched, but dared not utter a sound.

Terry Knorr, having seen more in her short life than most people twice her age, stood behind her mother in the entrance to the main bedroom. Her other sister, Sheila, in the doorway of the bathroom, begged Theresa Knorr to stop.

But neither the mother nor her sons took any notice. Then the two girls saw that their mother had something in her right hand, hanging limply down by the side of her enormous girth. It was a silver pistol with a black plastic handle; a small .22 derringer with a capacity of just two bullets. But one would be enough.

Suesan screamed as she caught sight of that weapon, clutched in her mother's pudgy, pink hands.

Suddenly the whole scene faded to slow motion. Terry watched as her mum lifted her arm and pointed the gun at her sister.

A pop like a champagne cork exploding was the only evidence that she had fired the gun straight at her daughter. The bullet entered underneath her left breast and went right through her rib cage before lodging itself in her back.

Terry watched her sister grab her chest, gasp, then clutch the doorframe of the bathroom before stumbling and then falling into the empty bathtub.

An eerie silence enveloped the house for a few seconds as the full impact of what had just occurred sank into the minds of all those present.

Theresa Knorr was the first one to snap out of that trance. She moved swiftly towards her injured daughter. Clinically, like the nurse she had once been, Theresa Knorr tried to rip the clothes off wounded Suesan. Then she pulled her daughter over the edge of the tub to examine the wound – her only concern was to see precisely where the bullet had entered the body.

That night, Terry and Sheila scrubbed the floor where Suesan had been shot. They scrubbed the doorframe where there were bloodstains. They scrubbed every inch of the bathroom apart from the tub where their sister still lay mortally wounded. Theresa Knorr did not have to tell them to do it. They just got on with the task at hand rather than face the wrath of their demonic mother.

Often, the kids would be up until two or three in the

morning scrubbing floors and hand-waxing. It was just part of life in that house.

Throughout their entire childhood Theresa Knorr had refused to allow any strangers in the house, because she did not want it dirtied up. In that bathroom, Theresa issued a dire warning to her brood of children: 'Just keep your mouths shut. If we have to get rid of the body, we will.'

Theresa Knorr was already referring to her daughter Suesan as though she were dead.

Terry wanted to go to the authorities to report the shooting incident, but she feared for her life, so she kept quiet.

Meanwhile, Suesan remained trapped in the bathtub. The other children would regularly creep into the bathroom and stand and stare at her.

Sheila was the one child who bothered to actually talk to her wounded sibling.

Theresa Knorr overheard one conversation between her two daughters during which Sheila spoke about suicide. Minutes later, Terry claims, Theresa Knorr did something that shocked even the boys.

She handed Sheila the very same gun she had just tried to murder her other daughter with, forced it into her shaking hand and said, 'If you're so depressed, then kill yourself.'

Sheila held tightly on to the gun. Perhaps it was the answer. She walked to her bedroom, lifted the gun to her head and squeezed the trigger. It had no bullets in it ...

Back in her bathroom prison, Suesan was still somehow surviving despite a massive loss of blood and only a pillow and 'a blanket for comfort. Amazingly, as the days turned to weeks, she even gradually began to regain her strength.

But the strangest aspect of this already bizarre scenario was that Theresa Knorr then began attending to her injured daughter as if she was the apple of her eye. Lovingly, she dabbed at the half-inch entrance wound where that bullet she had fired so coldly had pierced Suesan through to her back. She even patched the injury with gauze pads. And she regularly fed her daughter antibiotics to stop the infection from spreading. A liberal dose of Flexeril was provided from her secret store of medicines to stop the pain. The drugs all came from hospitals where Theresa had worked years previously.

Theresa could hardly be described as uncommunicative with her children either. She matter-of-factly informed them of the reasons why their sister had to remain in that hellhole of a bathtub. They had no choice, she told her clan. Theresa knew that, if there was blood left on anything, then it could easily be traced.

She also did not want to move her daughter, because she didn't know if the bullet would be dislodged. Terry later wondered if this was a sign of compassion on the part of her mother (or simply an effort to avoid any further spillages of blood).

But Terry did not doubt that, having cruelly shot her own daughter, Theresa Knorr turned into a caring nurse, regularly washing her injured daughter and tending to her wounds.

However, at the same time, she forbade the other children from sharing toilet facilities with Suesan by claiming they could catch a disease from her. The real Theresa Knorr was never far away.

As Theresa's clinical attitude continued to be tempered by the occasional sign of warmth, she even told Suesan that she was sorry and asked for forgiveness.

'I forgive you,' whispered Suesan.

That was one of many mistakes Suesan made. The beatings would never end.

As the weeks turned into a month, Suesan emerged from the bathroom having survived a bullet without receiving any professional medical attention. Theresa Knorr was doggedly determined to make sure the authorities never discovered anything about the shooting, even if it had almost cost her daughter her life.

Suesan became a virtual heroine in the eyes of her brothers and sisters. Whenever their mother was out of the room, she faced a stream of questions about the wound. Did the bullet hurt? Did you think you'd die? Terry was even allowed to touch the spot where the bullet had come to a halt after its almost fatal journey through Suesan's body. She could feel it still lodged in her sister's right side.

Theresa Knorr feared that Suesan might try to kill her in revenge for the shooting. She was also worried that her oldest son, Howard, would find out about the incident and decide to punish her. After years under his mother's control, Howard had made a new life for himself away from the ever growing web of physical and sexual abuse which now haunted Theresa Knorr and all her children.

She called Howard up within days of the shooting with a carefully concocted tale deliberately designed to throw him off the scent. Theresa Knorr told twenty-year-old Howard that Suesan had stabbed her sister Sheila with a steak knife. Sheila – under fear of punishment from her mother – backed up the story dutifully.

Theresa claimed to Howard that a few days later Sheila got hold of the derringer and shot Suesan. The mother reassured her son it had only been a surface wound and she had removed the bullet safely just a short time after the shooting.

Once Suesan had made a recovery – even though she still had the bullet lodged next to her ribs – she tried to keep out of the house on Bellingham Way as much as possible. Frequently she'd stay at friends' homes or remain out until late at night.

Howard and his common-law wife Connie moved back into the house when it was up for sale after the shooting. They noticed the scar on Suesan, but the entire family insisted the wound had been inflicted by Sheila, not her mother. Only those in the house on that fateful day knew the truth.

Even Suesan herself backed up this lie by insisting it had been her sister who shot her.

Connie was terrified by Theresa Knorr. One night when she and Howard were living by candlelight in the by-now deserted house in Orangevale, she heard a noise, opened the door to the hallway and there was Theresa Knorr emptying out a closet. Theresa turned to her and said, 'I know what you are. I know what you're doing. You will be punished. Your time will come.'

Connie's only two sins in the eyes of Theresa Knorr were to be younger and prettier than her *and* responsible for luring her oldest son away to a new life.

A few weeks later an even more chilling event convinced Connie to try and avoid setting foot inside the Knorr household whenever possible. She was pregnant with her first child by Howard when Theresa Knorr dropped in at Connie's mother's home, which she had moved back to, and informed Connie that Suesan had told her the baby was a boy, would be born on 1 February, and he would have a birth defect. All three prophecies came true.

Then Theresa repeated her earlier claims that Suesan had gained special powers after selling her soul to the devil. But, Theresa Knorr insisted, Suesan told her that she was going to kill Connie and the baby because there were not supposed to be any more descendants to carry on the family name. Connie was petrified. She had found herself involved in a very dangerous family.

FIVE

'What did you do that made all of us turn
out so well?'

JOHN WESLEY, IN A LETTER TO HIS MOTHER SUZANNA

'I beat the devil out of you all.'

SUZANNA WESLEY'S REPLY

When Theresa Knorr and her tribe of children moved out of the house in Orangevale to take up residence in a rented cottage just off Auburn Boulevard, on the outskirts of north Sacramento, all the youngsters hoped that it might mark a new violence-free phase in the Knorr household.

The move itself, on 3 October 1983, initiated a reunion between Theresa and her estranged sister Rosemary, whose husband Floyd Norris helped the boys load their U-Haul truck to the brim with furniture for the move to the new place. For years the two sisters had refused to have any contact with each other. No one in the family knew the specific reasons for the feud, but then there had been so many weird incidents over the years it could have been any of a dozen things.

The single-storey property on Auburn was really an annex to the two-storey apartment block it was attached to, and many of the residents on that block and in the trailers scattered nearby referred to it as the 'laundry room'. But the sale of the house in Orangevale had enabled Theresa Knorr to walk away with $50,000 profit, and she was not about to fritter it away on some fancy home. At $280-a-month rent, the Auburn house was a bargain.

Other children on the block soon got to know the Knorr kids, and some were surprised by their attitude towards their mother when her back was turned.

Billy Bob frequently described his mother as nutty and weird to neighbour William Hall. And Theresa Knorr showed herself to have a distinct lack of a sense of humour after Hall stopped to pass the time of day with her and somehow ended up getting around to the subject of Adam and Eve. When Hall joked, 'That was a classic case of incest,' Theresa Knorr walked off in a huff, obviously deeply offended.

But within a few months Theresa Knorr made up with the Halls and became quite friendly with the young family. She even gave them a painting of a fountain scene for Christmas. The Halls – suspicious that there might bean underlying influence of satanism inside the Knorr household – became convinced the picture was in some way cursed, and eventually Bill's wife made him take it off the wall because she believed it would bring them bad luck.

Suesan – the bullet still firmly lodged in her back – was still trying to keep out of her mother's way, but life proved even more terrifying for her inside the new house. Theresa Knorr had deliberately chosen a smaller property so she could keep an even closer eye on her clan. She was especially determined to control every aspect of Suesan's life. Since the shooting, Theresa had continued to decide when and where her daughter should eat. She was banned from joining the others at mealtimes for days on end.

Within a few days of the family moving into the house just off Auburn Boulevard, Theresa Knorr produced a pair of police regulation handcuffs bought at a pawnshop at nearby Del Paso Boulevard and ordered Suesan to put socks over her hands so the manacles would not leave any marks on her wrists. Later, she introduced canvas wrist restraints because, despite the preventative measures, definite marks could be seen on Suesan's wrists.

Suesan complied with her mother's orders because she knew she would be beaten either by her mother or brother Billy Bob if she disobeyed.

Theresa Knorr also regularly blindfolded Suesan with a silk scarf from her vast selection of scarves, collected since the early seventies, when they were considered fashionable.

Suesan was the child most feared by Theresa Knorr. She was still regularly muttering about her daughter being sent by the devil, and she always insisted that at least one of the other children stand guard over her. They were told that, if Suesan got out of the house, they were in big trouble, and they knew what that meant.

Theresa Knorr's other main motive for keeping Suesan

prisoner was to prevent her repeating that previous trip she had made to the Child Protection Services in Sacramento.

Once, when Theresa went on a rare shopping trip with her newfound fortune from selling the house in Orangevale, Terry was left at home with Suesan and her brother Robert. Theresa had not fed Suesan for a couple of days and she was weak. Terry went into the kitchen and got her a glass of water with sugar in it so that it would help bring her blood sugar back up. Diabetes ran in the family, and Terry thought that her sister might have been diabetic. Also, there was no food in the house, so she could not give her anything more substantial.

Talk of black magic and Suesan's so-called dangerous powers continued to dominate Theresa Knorr's conversation inside the house off Auburn Boulevard. None of the children dared question their mother's rantings. By this time, Terry recalls, Suesan was so battered and bruised by her mother and brothers that her appearance was physically altered. In the eyes of her family, that was yet more evidence of the devil within her.

After handcuffing her to her bed each night, Theresa Knorr allegedly fed her daughter Mellaril tranquillisers to keep her sedated to prevent her from getting hysterical.

At night the other children lay terrified in their beds as weird voices emanated from Suesan. There were dozens of different tones and accents; deep, throaty roars; high-pitched screams; constant mumbling in Spanish. It was more like a scene out of *The Exorcist* than family life in a suburban California town.

Theresa Knorr told the others that Suesan had to be locked up, as she was trying to kill her sister Sheila because she was a virgin and she wanted to use Sheila for a human sacrifice.

And, Theresa insisted, Suesan was still sometimes – feeding her huge doses of sleeping pills in her drinks at night, and she believed she was going to try and kill her. Theresa was also convinced that her daughter's illness had caused her own excessive weight gain, intestinal problems, stomach aches, headaches and high blood pressure. She insisted Suesan was deliberately making her sick because she had signed her name in blood and sold her soul to the devil.

To the outside world, Theresa Knorr's ailments sound more like the classic symptoms of hypochondria. But in that household no one ever questioned her words of wisdom.

Murders in the sprawling blue-collar suburbs of Sacramento are not all that rare, so the violent, tragic death of Theresa Knorr's sister Rosemary on 30 November 1983, caused no more than a ripple of interest in the city.

Inside the Knorr household off Auburn Boulevard it was very much the same story. It was as if the brutality that ruled the lives of Theresa Knorr and her flock of children had neutralised any real emotions when it came to anything that happened outside those four walls.

The *Sacramento Bee* daily newspaper followed police enquiries into Rosemary Norris's murder in the suburb of

Roseville with only a sprinkling of interest. Reading between the lines of the newspaper's published reports, it seemed as if her demise was considered a low-life trailer-trash-type crime. Who cared?

A piece on page 6 headlined INVESTIGATORS FINALLY IDENTIFY WOMAN STRANGLED IN PLACER on 2 December 1983, seemed to say it all:

AUBURN – The Placer County Sheriff's Department identified Thursday the strangled woman whose body was left on a dead-end road in southern Placer County as Rosemary Morris, 39, of Citrus Heights.

An autopsy Thursday found that Morris died of 'manual strangulation,' Sheriff Don Nunes said.

A Rocklin man found the body while walking his dog in the Sunset-Whitney industrial area between Roseville and Rocklin, Nunes said.

Investigators found no tracks or any sign there had been a struggle at the scene. 'Her body temperature (when found) would suggest that she was only recently deposited there,' Nunes said.

Officials are looking for a missing 1967 white-and-blue GMC truck which belonged to Norris.

But, despite the *Bee*'s low-key projection of the murder, homicide detectives were naturally determined to find the killer.

Rosemary Norris had last been seen by friends at her Castillo Court home at 4.30 p.m. on the day she disappeared.

Unlike her lazier, younger sister, she had worked for many years at the state's Department of Finance headquarters in Sacramento. She was the success story of the family.

Her husband, Floyd Norris Jr., had reported Rosemary missing to the Sacramento County Sheriff's Department when he returned home the following day from a business trip.

Privately, detectives suspected who might be responsible for the killing, but they needed more evidence before they could even consider issuing an arrest warrant.

'Do you mind if I come in to ask you a few questions about the death of your sister?'

Detective Johnnie Smith had a hunch that Theresa Knorr might know something about her sister's killing, so he called at the house just off Auburn Boulevard, in mid-December 1983.

The detective suspected there might have been some sort of relationship between Rosemary's husband and Theresa because he had been spending a lot of time at the house.

Smith did not notice anything wrong inside that house when he sat down in the living room to interview Theresa Knorr. He saw all the children, except Suesan. And Theresa Knorr even struck him as a caring mother.

Theresa was charming to the visiting policeman. She told Smith a sob story about how her sister considered her the black sheep of the family because she had been married so many times. Smith never once heard Suesan Knorr whimpering, and he certainly had no idea she may have been manacled to a table in the kitchen while he was in the house.

The only thing that stuck in the detective's mind was that Theresa Knorr looked very strange, with her black, greasy hair down to her waist and very overweight. But he also noted the children were coming and going in a relaxed manner.

'I have thought about this so many times since,' he said many years later. 'I thought about whether there was something I should have detected. Was there some problem? But I was there on an entirely different matter.'

Smith left the house that day none the wiser as far as his investigation into the murder of Rosemary Norris was concerned. Theresa Knorr had tactfully answered all his questions, but provided him with no fresh clues as to the identity of the killer.

Three months later, in mid-March 1984, two men sitting in their four-door sedan did not even merit a glance in the busy roadway that led to the apartment block attached to the house, just off Auburn Boulevard.

They watched four of the Knorr children coming and going without even questioning the fact that one daughter never seemed to emerge from the house. But then that was not the purpose of the Placer County Sheriff's Department surveillance operation.

Their job was to observe the movements of Floyd Norris Jr. following his wife's mysterious death. It was a last-ditch effort to try and pin the murder on the husband. They were still intrigued by his continual visits to his sister-in-law's home. Perhaps they were having an affair, as police had suspected months earlier? Or maybe they were involved in some business scheme or other? Whatever the reasons behind Norris's trips to Auburn Boulevard, Detective Johnnie Smith wanted some answers and, since Floyd was not talking, a watching and waiting game was their only option.

For more than three days Smith and his partner observed Floyd's movements, completely unaware of the fear and injury being inflicted by Theresa Knorr on her children inside that very house. As it happened, antique dealer and furniture restorer Norris was reupholstering some chairs for his sister-in-law, and that seems to have been the only motive behind his regular visits. Unknown to everyone at the time, Theresa Knorr had had another falling out with her sister just a few weeks before her murder, following a row concerning some money Rosemary had loaned to her sister. But Theresa was not and never has been a suspect in the death of Rosemary Norris.

Detective Smith later conceded that Floyd Norris had been a suspect, but detectives never uncovered any evidence that would pin it on him.

Floyd Norris moved away to Reno, Nevada, sometime after his wife's death, and police have completely lost track of him.

SIX

Whoever strikes his father or mother
shall be put to death.

EXODUS 21:15

With the arrival of spring, life inside that small house off Auburn Boulevard continued to go from bad to worse for Theresa Knorr's daughters.

Terry remembers that by this time her mother was convinced that not only had Suesan given her a fatal illness, but also that her daughter was suffering from venereal disease, which Theresa Knorr was in danger of catching if she did not take certain preventative measures.

Just after the police surveillance of the house ended, Theresa Knorr decided to ban Suesan from sharing the same toilet with the rest of the family for fear of getting VD from her. Unlike the house at Bellingham, there was only one toilet in their new home.

Suesan continued to be handcuffed to her bed each night. Theresa Knorr tended to make the manacles doubly tight on evenings when there was a full moon, according to the other children.

Gradually, the energy and health that Suesan had battled so bravely to regain following that shooting the previous year was being drained out of her body. Theresa Knorr seemed to take a perverse delight in watching her daughter slowly disintegrate in front of her very eyes. The move to Auburn Boulevard was in effect the final nail in Suesan Knorr's coffin …

One night, Theresa Knorr made Suesan stand with her back to her in the tiny kitchen. Suesan was so sick with fever by this stage that she was virtually a walking zombie, too weak to argue with anybody about anything.

Theresa Knorr allegedly picked up a pair of scissors and aimed them at her daughter's back as if she were about to throw a dart into a board. The scissors embedded at least an inch into their target. Suesan stood there in silence, and Theresa looked admiringly at her handiwork. A few moments later she pulled them out of her daughter's back without a word, treated the wound with gauze padding and then ordered her to her bedroom, where she was handcuffed and blindfolded once more. Naturally, there would be no calls to doctors, no professional medical advice. Theresa Knorr would take care of it all. And no one ever dared ask her what the sick and twisted reason behind that attack had been.

It was exactly the same story a few weeks later when she stood on Suesan's neck as punishment for some sin or other. Youngest sister Terry watched as Suesan – convulsing on the floor – was crushed underfoot by Theresa Knorr's enormous frame.

Susan Sullivan – who lived in the apartment block attached to the Knorr house – took pity on young Terry and regularly let her come to her apartment to watch television.

But two incidents occurred that sparked some problems. The first was when Terry visited Susan's apartment one day, and a few hours later Susan noticed a pair of earrings missing.

She went to speak to Theresa Knorr about the missing items, and shortly afterwards Theresa came back up to Susan's apartment and gave her another pair of earrings, which clearly implied that the others had been stolen by Terry.

But Susan Sullivan was even more concerned when the attractive teenager started flirting with a male friend of hers, who was eighty years old.

'She started to get real over-chummy with this guy. It got to the point where I started to say, 'hold on there, young lady''', explained Susan. 'I decided there and then I did not want her around any more. I did not trust her. Maybe it was the lack of a father around the house that made her so overfriendly with my guy. But she kept brushing against him, smiling at him real seductively and flirting with him the whole time. In the end I just gave her and the rest of the family the cold shoulder.'

A few miles away across town – on 1 June 1984 – Theresa

Knorr's oldest son, Howard, married live-in lover Connie, but, sadly, they were not destined to live happily ever after. Their relationship was in trouble even before the wedding.

Connie believes her marriage to Howard was ruined by his mother's influence because he attempted to exert the same type of control over her. Connie says she suffered numerous beatings at the hands of her abusive ex-husband. He even spent a year in jail for one attack in the late 1980s.

Connie filed a list of incidents with spousal abuse agencies in Sacramento, including when she alleged Howard beat his baby son, Howard Jr., before going out on a drug run. Soon after, she fled the house they shared, filed divorce proceedings and sought full custody of their two children.

In 1990, Howard was arrested after making threats to hire someone to kill his wife. Connie says she dropped the charges after getting scared: She also claimed that Howard boasted to her about beating a boy when he was a youngster at school.

To Connie, Howard had become like a robot on behalf of his mother. Even after the Knorrs moved out of that house on Bellingham, Theresa would call Howard every time she had a problem with the children and ask him to come over and help teach them a lesson.

The fifth of July 1984 was one of those rare evenings when there was no screaming, no abuse, no stabbings, and no shootings inside the Knorr household. The atmosphere was about as laid-back as anyone could remember. The lull before the storm . . .

The main cause of all this, according to Terry, was the pungent whiff of cannabis that wafted across the living room of the cottage. Sitting on a couch, like two giggling students, were Theresa Knorr and Suesan, the daughter she had abused so horrifically.

Taking an enormous drag of the fat, badly rolled joint, Theresa Knorr gazed almost lovingly at her battered daughter before exhaling a vast cloud of mustardy smoke.

Daughter Terry, just thirteen years old at the time, watched her mother and sister taking those illicit drugs, convinced it was proof that perhaps her mother still had some sense of reality left in her mind. It was ironic that mind-altering substances might actually be responsible for cleansing Theresa Knorr's soul ... albeit temporarily.

Terry was amazed that her mother and Suesan – the object of so many vicious attacks – were actually talking together like a mother and daughter should. Suesan was yet again playing her role as the ultimate human sponge, prepared to soak up vicious attacks and virtually constant imprisonment, in exchange for the very occasional evidence of a loving, caring mother.

The cannabis also persuaded Suesan to make one last desperate attempt to escape her hellhole. It was anaesthetising all that pain so much that she managed to beg her mother to let her leave home. Anything. Any life outside that house seemed preferable to what she had just gone through.

'Just buy me a plane ticket, send me to Alaska. I'll be a

prostitute on the pipeline. I don't care, I just wanna leave,' a very stoned Suesan told her mother.

Equally stoned, Theresa Knorr actually allowed the pot to mellow her rigidity. She announced she'd allow her daughter to leave home – but there was one condition. Suesan would have to let her mother remove that bullet still lodged in her back.

Through the clouds of cannabis smoke it seemed a reasonable request. For the first time since being shot, Suesan could see just a glint of light at the end of that awful tunnel. Having that bullet removed was going to be Suesan's ticket to freedom.

The reason Theresa insisted on taking out the bullet before freeing her daughter, Terry later told police, was because she knew it was evidence of the crime she had committed against her daughter. She was afraid she could be traced by the bullet. Some years earlier her guns had been taken by the police and ballistic tests done on them, and she believed they could be traced back to her.

One of the detectives investigating the Knorr case ten years later asked Terry what would have happened if Suesan had just got up and walked out of that house.

'Suesan would have ended up dead,' came the cold reply.

The surgery to remove Suesan's bullet, as described by Terry, resembled a scene out of *Frankenstein*. Terry played the role of doctor's assistant, but in reality her job was more like anaesthetist/assistant surgeon/nurse all wrapped into one.

However, this was no operating theatre. This was the kitchen of a tiny, overcrowded house, and there was not even a gurney in sight. Instead, just a slab of floor where Suesan was told to lie in preparation for her surgery. A pillow was placed under her stomach so that it would be taut enough for surgery to commence.

A couple of medical instruments lay idly nearby on the sideboard. Suesan was fed a handful of tiny green Mellaril painkillers, but it was a gallon bottle of Old Crow whisky that would become the Knorr equivalent of anaesthetic.

Before positioning her daughter for what in anyone's terms was major surgery, Theresa Knorr thrust that vast jug of whiskey into her daughter's lap and ordered her to drink it. Unlike the macaroni cheese all those months earlier, this was one command that Suesan believed was actually in her own interests.

Suesan rapidly swallowed back about half of the Old Crow before she was knocked out cold.

Meanwhile, Theresa smoothed on a pair of rubber surgical gloves, making sure to stretch them professionally before squeezing them over those short, stubby fingers. She ordered her two sons, Billy Bob and Robert, to hold their sister down. Then she grabbed a scalpel and a pair of pincers, and got to work. She had stolen everything from her earlier jobs in convalescent hospitals.

Two hours later Theresa finally succeeded in digging the bullet out of her daughter's back. Suesan lost enormous quantities of blood, but that did not seem to concern her mother. Her main objective was to remove the evidence that could have resulted in her being prosecuted for attempted murder.

From the moment she extracted that slug, she clung on to it, not even daring to set it down for a second, in case it disappeared. She did not trust any of her children – she suspected they would turn her in if given half a chance.

Suesan was still knocked out cold. Her face was twisted to the side; pressed hard on the cold kitchen floor. Her back arched at a grotesque angle. Somehow she was still breathing.

Theresa said nothing. Her assistant, Terry, was so dumbfounded that she could not speak …

Luckily for Suesan, she did not recover consciousness until the next day. Although some members of the family believe that she would have been better off if she had never woken up.

When Suesan did awake, she was still severely groggy and her body remained facedown on the floor, growing weaker and more feverish with each passing hour. Theresa Knorr ordered the other children to simply step around or over Suesan whenever they were in the kitchen.

She would not even allow the rest of the family to help Suesan to the bathroom. Theresa Knorr simply ordered Billy Bob and Robert to place nappies beneath Suesan's pelvis and change them when the smell of urine and faeces got too overpowering in the summer heat.

Theresa fed her daughter constant antibiotics to keep infection from setting in, and she gave her ibuprofen and Motrin for the inflammation.

But Suesan was deteriorating fast. A week after the operation, she started hallucinating and began calling her brother William, 'Grandpa.'

'I can see my life passing before my eyes,' Suesan told her baby sister Terry.

Then lockjaw set in . . .

'She was dying. I just know,' says Terry today. 'It was like a movie, you know ...'

The other sister, Sheila, was so concerned she actually plucked up the courage to confront her mother, 'Suesan's dying. We gotta do something.'

'What d'you want me to do about it? I've tried to help her. There's nothing more I can do,' came the terse reply from the only parent in that household.

Theresa Knorr allegedly conceded that her daughter did need proper medical attention, but she strictly forbade any attempt to call in a doctor, for fear it would expose her. When she wanted to see if Suesan was still alive, she kicked her and listened for a groan.

'She needs a doctor, she needs to go to a hospital, but, if I take her to a hospital, she's been beaten so badly that I'm gonna go to jail. We can't do that.'

The children were told to sit with their sister and keep an eye on her all night long.

SEVEN

'When the child recovers from the attack, he feels
enormously confused, in fact, split – innocent
and culpable at the same time – and the confidence
in the testimony of his own senses is broken.
To survive this ordeal, the child has to register
the bad … as good.'

ALBERT SHENGOLD, CHILD CARE EXPERT

On the evening of July 12, 1984, Theresa Knorr walked into the children's bedroom, sat down on one of the bunk beds, and announced to her sons and Sheila that she had come up with a solution on what to do with Suesan, who was still sprawled out on the kitchen floor. Her wound had become so badly infected that the skin had turned pink, then bright red all around the gaping sore.

Terry – keeping guard over Suesan in the kitchen – could not avoid staring at her sister's eyes. Her adolescent curiosity was getting the better of her. Suesan's once pretty, sparkling blue eyes had transformed to a pale, yellowing greenish colour in a matter of days.

Theresa Knorr later told one family member that her daughter's change of eye colour had been caused by the devil. She told her daughter-in-law Connie that Suesan was definitely a witch. She insisted that the only way to kill a witch was to burn them.

As Terry stared at her sister, her eyes panned down and noticed a rib almost poking through Suesan's stomach and hundreds of black marks on her back.

With just an undersized nappy around her waist, Suesan Knorr was actually experiencing less dignity in life than death.

The following day, Theresa Knorr began her preparations for the scheme she had been planning with Sheila and the boys. First she went and bought a red, one-gallon petrol can. Then she filled her son's yellow 1978 Mercury Cougar – known around the Knorr household as the 'pimp mobile' – with petrol.

Terry watched her mother pack the petrol can in the boot of the Mercury, together with a large box of six-inch-long Blue Diamond wooden matches. She also saw Theresa put all of Suesan's belongings into a plastic Glad rubbish bag and load that into the car as well; clothes, jewellery, purses, belts, shoes.

The final proof of what was about to happen came when Terry witnessed her mother performing an extraordinary ritual in the yard behind the house.

'I watched her take olive oil. It was her little God ritual thing. She took olive oil, poured it over my sister's pictures. She pulled every picture she had of my sister, and she burned them,' Terry later explained.

Back inside the house, Suesan was being dressed up by her brothers and sister Sheila. They put her clothes on her like a toddler being prepared for school. First they struggled to get her into a dark-coloured corduroy jumpsuit with a hood. Then followed white sneakers and a ski-jacket-style coat.

It was past midnight on 15 July when Theresa Knorr, her two sons and her daughter Sheila were finally ready to depart. Youngest daughter Terry pleaded desperately with her mother to be allowed to join them on their trip. Theresa had already admitted she was going to get rid of Suesan. The boys told her they were going to set her alight somewhere in the mountains.

Terry feared being left alone in the house. But Theresa rejected her pleas. She did not want her youngest daughter to see the sacrifice of her sister.

'Loose lips sink ships,' she told Terry.

In the background, groaning on the kitchen floor, was helpless Suesan, a constant stream of incoherent babbling coming from between her lips.

Just before they took her out, Terry leaned down and whispered in her sister's ear, *'I love you.'*

In another room, Theresa Knorr was getting the car keys and her bag as if she was rushing out to get to the local store before it closed.

Robert and William crouched down on either side of Suesan and pulled her up, holding her arms: Suesan had drop foot and they had to drag her across the floor, her feet hanging limply behind her. She wasn't even attempting to walk.

Terry was then ordered to hold the front seat of the two-door car forward while they stuck Suesan in the backseat. Her head slumped on to Sheila's lap and then her knees were pulled over Robert's lap. It was one hell of a squash by all accounts, as the Cougar was not a big car. Up front Billy Bob and his mother, who drove, sank into the bucket seats.

Terry watched as the Cougar purred off along the narrow track towards the exit from the trailer-park complex, and then she returned to the empty house terrified. Fear and paranoia ran rampant through her confused mind.

Two hours later the distinct rumble of the Cougar's V8 alerted Terry that her family had returned. Theresa Knorr walked in mumbling something about the engine in William's car knocking. Their plan had been aborted at the last moment. Suesan Knorr's death sentence had been commuted ... for a few hours at least. She was returned to her miserable home on the kitchen floor, too delirious to realise that the family had already agreed to restart their mission the following evening.

Theresa Knorr and Billy Bob announced they were exhausted following their late-night excursion, and retired for a nap in the bunk beds in the children's room. Theresa, far too heavy to manage to clamber up to the top bunk, took the bottom bed.

Billy Bob, as Terry always called him, hardly ever got spanked by his mother. Theresa Knorr's blatant favouritism towards him was the result of Billy Bob's remarkable resemblance to how Robert Knorr Sr. looked when he was in the Marines and first swept Theresa off her feet.

Early the next evening, the brothers were ordered to transfer all Suesan's belongings to Theresa's car, a maroon 1978 Ford LTD with a white vinyl top. It was a strange-looking vehicle, a two-door sedan in the body of a four-door limo, complete with wire spoke wheels and whitewall tyres. Terry never forgot those whitewall tyres because her mother made her clean and polish the scruffy car so perfectly.

That night, Terry was once again ordered to play the role of prison guard on Suesan as she lay dying on the kitchen floor. At one point during the evening, the terrified thirteen-year-old actually thought her sister had died. She got down next to the body on her knees and shook her and talked to her. At first there was no response. She repeated her actions. Suesan started babbling nonsense again. It was like music to Terry's ears because it meant she was still alive.

Terry continued her round-the-clock guard duty until about midnight, when the family plan was reignited. This time Terry did not plead to join them. Her instincts told her it would be better not to play any part in their dreadful scheme.

Theresa Knorr carefully reversed the car along the side of the house before they carried Suesan out of the back door dressed in the same jumpsuit. They placed her in exactly the same position in the Ford LTD as they had in the Cougar the previous evening.

Terry studied her brothers and sisters for any signs of emotion. Robert seemed really twitchy, while Billy Bob was calm and cool, showing no fear. Theresa Knorr was the same. But Sheila was shaking.

Theresa and her clan drove up Interstate 80, northeast towards Reno. About sixty miles out of Sacramento, just beyond the Dormer Pass, Theresa turned south on state Highway 89 and headed for the winter ski resort of Squaw Valley. In the summer months it wasn't nearly so popular, and it didn't take long to find a secluded spot near Squaw Creek. There, they unloaded the pile of Suesan's belongings and fashioned a makeshift bier. They set Suesan on top of it. Then Billy Bob doused her with generous amounts of petrol. Theresa Knorr waddled back to the car and started the engine. She watched as her son lit a match and dropped it on the bier and ran back to the car.

'If you ever tell anybody about this, you're going to be next,' Theresa told Billy Bob as he climbed back into the Ford LTD.

The drive back to Auburn Boulevard at dawn that morning was carried out in virtually complete silence. But one incident occurred that terrified Theresa and her children more than the murder of their own flesh and blood.

Suddenly, as they powered along Highway 89, a bird smashed into the windscreen of the Ford LTD, almost shattering it. Theresa was so thrown by the incident she swerved the car dangerously and almost lost control. Sheila was screaming. All the occupants of the car that sweltering night were convinced of one thing – that bird had committed suicide on the windscreen. Theresa Knorr told her children it was a sign – 'an offering or a sacrifice'.

They presumed the bird was the soul of Suesan come to say goodbye forever.

The following morning, 17 July, the family returned to the house off Auburn Boulevard minus Suesan. Theresa Knorr and her sons were keen to tell little Terry all the graphic details. They told her how they left Suesan in a beautiful area that was surrounded by trees, and there was a little clearing, like a meadow, as if to reassure her that her sister's final resting place was so pretty it was the perfect place to die.

Theresa explained to Terry how Billy Bob pulled Suesan out of the car, laid her down, then, with Robert, pulled all her belongings out and spread them all around her. Robert then got back in the car, where Sheila sat terrified.

'When they poured gas over her and they got to about her chest area, her lower face area, it was like her entire body just collapsed, just like her soul was leaving her body,' Terry recalled them telling her.

Theresa even reassured Terry that her sister had already died before the blaze was started.

'That's when her soul escaped the corpse,' she chillingly added.

Howard Sanders – the only member of Theresa Knorr's family to have actually escaped the nest before the death of Suesan – read an article in the *Bee* about a body found burning near Tahoe City just a few days later. It instantly reminded his wife Connie of those chilling conversations with her mother-in-law some weeks earlier when she had talked about having Suesan exorcised.

Howard carefully studied every word of the article, which

reported that authorities had found the body off Highway 89 and presumed it was a woman who had a child because of the nappies scattered near the body. Howard suspected it must have been his half-sister.

Howard confronted his mother on the phone, but she just said, simply, that Suesan had gone. Howard, understandably stunned, tried to question his mother further, but she repeated that she had gone. When he pressed her once again, she admitted Suesan was dead, but refused to elaborate. Instead she promised her oldest son she would tell him about it some other time.

When Howard next saw his mother, she insisted that Suesan had died of natural causes. But she refused to go into much detail. Howard did not believe his mother, and later confronted his two brothers, Robert and Billy Bob, about the article in the *Bee*. Robert admitted the body referred to was Suesan but added cryptically: 'She was literally rotting away alive anyhow.'

When Howard was living with his in-laws in Pershing Avenue, Orangevale, Theresa Knorr dropped by un-expectedly one afternoon and insisted her son go in the Ford LTD with her.

Howard was terrified of his mother because of what he suspected had happened to Suesan. He was afraid that she might kill him if he asked too many questions about Suesan.

Howard was particularly spooked by the menacing-looking pair of tight red leather driving gloves his mother was wearing when she picked him up that day. Red was her favourite colour. He was convinced she was using them to avoid getting her fingerprints on anything.

Paranoia was running rampant through Theresa Knorr's family – much of it fuelled by her brutal regime.

Shortly after Suesan's death, Terry, just thirteen, made the first of many attempts to run away from the dreadful place she called home. She took off to live with a gang of youths in their late teens in a run-down apartment block a short distance from Auburn Boulevard. Theresa Knorr was furious when she heard, and immediately ordered eldest son Howard to go and get her back with the aid of his younger brother, Billy Bob.

The two brothers went over to the building on Marconi where they had heard Terry was staying, to find a party in full swing. Howard banged on the door and heard Terry say, 'Oh shit, it's my brother.' She then ran out the back door, and a bunch of heavyset bikers rushed out the front and tried to pick a fight with Howard and Billy Bob.

Howard cooled the potentially dangerous situation by talking to the men, but he never actually persuaded Terry to come home. However, a few weeks later she arrived back at the house off Auburn Boulevard and all was forgiven ... for the time being.

EIGHT

'There's a light above me. I think it's a hole.
I'm gonna climb toward it.'

SHEILA SANDERS, THREE DAYS BEFORE SHE DIED

The seventeenth of February 1985 was a bleak and chilly night on Fulton Avenue, in the Del Paso Heights area of Sacramento. Tatty mid-seventies petrol guzzlers cruised close to the pavement with their full beams turned up to highlight the prostitutes advertising their bodies in exchange for the cost of a set of retreads. Their lights illuminated black leather skirts, assorted stilettos and white knee-high boots on a three-inch heel. But, whatever the packaging, the end result was the same.

Theresa Knorr's twenty-year-old daughter Sheila allegedly had only recently started working Fulton Avenue after some heavy pressure from her mother. Theresa demanded that each of her surviving children give her most of their earnings from whatever jobs – legal or illegal – they might have.

No one knows what Sheila really thought about working as a prostitute. It just wasn't a topic of conversation inside the Knorr household. When Theresa Knorr demanded that she pay her keep, Sheila at first started streetwalking on Auburn Boulevard, just two minutes from their house. But the clients who drifted along that red-light district rarely paid more than ten dollars a trick. The good money was over at Fulton. Word on the street was that car salesmen and the businessmen who owned the dozens of trailer parks in the area would happily pay as much as two hundred bucks for a few hours in a nearby motel room with a girl.

Youngest daughter Terry could not understand why her half-sister did not run away once she had earned some cash from turning tricks on Fulton. Terry certainly would have left home given half the chance. In her mind, getting up to $200 for each trick was the sort of big money that would provide a route out of that terrible household.

Life inside Theresa Knorr's home was also difficult for Sheila for other reasons. She did not want to be a prostitute forever, and she was dating one local guy seriously, even considering marriage. But she could not ask her boyfriend back to the house – let alone mention the word marriage in front of her mother – without risking a terrible beating.

Sheila regularly ended up with two black eyes following a thrashing by Theresa and her boys. But Sheila did not once attempt to run away – however unpleasant life became, she seemed to stay out of some misplaced loyalty towards the family:

Meanwhile, Theresa Knorr had banned the very mention of deceased daughter Suesan after becoming occasionally and uncharacteristically haunted by her memory. Theresa admitted sometimes feeling a cold draft up her back when she walked past Suesan's closet. She believed that her daughter's soul had come back to haunt her.

However, police would later charge that none of this stopped Theresa Knorr from turning her brutal attentions towards Sheila. One day she beat her up after accusing her of getting pregnant by one of the many men who paid her for sex over at Fulton.

Over the next few weeks, Theresa Knorr became increasingly obsessed about Sheila's 'pregnancy', even though there was no actual evidence she was expecting a child.

Things reached a head late one night when Theresa made Sheila cycle to the shop more than half a mile away on Auburn Boulevard, to pick up some cigarettes.

Cycling furiously past the leery eyes of the transvestites and rent boys plying for trade on the strip of Auburn known as the 'meat rack', Sheila must have wondered where her life was leading. There was no escape from Sacramento's thriving cash-for-sex scene, even while out on an errand for her mother.

But, as she pedalled past the imposing entrance to the Lombard Mortuary, a motorist rammed into her bike, knocking her to the ground. The driver did not even stop to see if she was OK. But then that was typical of life on the rougher side of town.

Sheila was taken by paramedics to the nearby Mercy Hospital, in Sacramento. For once the bruises and cuts had not been inflicted at home, but any hope that Theresa Knorr might actually offer some sympathy soon disappeared.

Her mother was concerned about the accident. But her worries had nothing to do with Sheila's injuries. She believed that the incident was a sign from above. A sign that indicated her daughter had been taken over by the devil.

Theresa was convinced that, when Sheila was hit in front of that mortuary, she had died and a demon took over her body, or so she told the rest of the family. However, there was worse to come.

Theresa still believed that Sheila was pregnant. That combination of twisted opinions sparked a tirade of abuse that was even more horrendous than anything Suesan had suffered the previous year before her death.

Within minutes of struggling back into the house from the hospital, Sheila was being held by her brothers Billy Bob and Robert while her mother gave her a serious beating.

Theresa Knorr, once of the delicate chin and wispy brown hair, was certainly no longer slender and easy on the eyes. She weighed 250 pounds and had her hair pulled back like a sumo wrestler. Her features were bloated. Her arms were the size of Popeye's, and her once-slim waistline was now as thick and elastic as a truck tyre. And she packed enormous power in each of those punches.

Sheila's body soon turned black and blue from where Theresa had beaten and strangled her. The nightmare was back on course, and that evening's proceedings had only just begun.

According to Terry, after smashing Sheila around for a while, Theresa Knorr started force-feeding Sheila with macaroni cheese, just as she had done to Suesan. Some old habits never die, they come back to haunt you forever.

On that same horrendous night, Theresa also managed to break Sheila's front tooth off while trying to force-feed her the macaroni. As the food was shovelled down her throat, she even started vomiting.

Theresa then decided that measures needed to be taken to prevent anyone from seeing some of her daughter's dreadful injuries. She forced Sheila to sit in the bathtub while she filled it with cold water and ice cubes. Then she made her stay in it for upwards of an hour in an effort to bring out the bruising she had just inflicted on her daughter.

From then on Theresa Knorr also began handcuffing Sheila to the underneath of the kitchen table at night so she could not escape. They were the same cuffs that had been used to such chilling effect on her sister less than a year earlier.

As an afterthought, Theresa called up lawyer Wes Seegmiller to help push for a claim off the insurance company following Sheila's accident. Theresa Knorr never liked to miss out on an opportunity to make some extra cash.

But another matter was particularly aggravating Theresa at that time. Her beloved teenage son Billy Bob had dared to announce he was leaving home to move into an apartment on run-down Fulton Boulevard with a pretty teenage girl called Emily Lewis, who worked with him at the cinema on Ethan Way.

Theresa was infuriated that her favourite son was striking out on his own. Billy Bob told dark-haired Emily that he had been kicked out of home by his mum – nothing could have been further from the truth. But, whatever his excuse, Billy Bob managed to persuade Emily to set up home with him, and he even took on another part-time job at Arco Arena and did a third job at a book company in West Sacramento to ensure he could afford the rent on the apartment.

Emily never went into the Knorr family home just off Auburn throughout the nine months she lived with Billy Bob. He told her that one of his sisters had run away and he openly admitted he did not care much for either Sheila or Suesan. Emily never questioned why Billy Bob was so obsessed with not allowing her inside the family house. She did feel there was something unusual about the family, and it worried her, but she could not actually fathom what the problem was.

With Theresa Knorr's obsession about Sheila's pregnancy growing every day, her eldest daughter was unshackled and allowed to go – under the escort of her two brothers, naturally – to a local doctor to establish once and for all if she was actually expecting a child.

When it was confirmed that she wasn't pregnant, Theresa still continued to insist Sheila had venereal disease. So she made her go to another doctor to be checked for chlamydia and pelvic inflammatory disease.

Theresa Knorr even took her own penicillin to fight off the diseases she was convinced she had caught from her daughter. She then started claiming to the other children that Sheila had secretly obtained a cure for her venereal disease and was deliberately not telling her.

One day, Theresa became so angry about this that she hog-tied Sheila in a cupboard across from the back bedroom of the apartment as punishment for her alleged deception.

Sheila had, in the eyes of her mother, given her venereal disease and then would not admit she had been cured of it. Theresa began to ration Sheila's food and refused to let her out of the cupboard.

At the end of May 1985, Theresa completely banned Sheila from being fed anything. She remained crammed in that tiny closet next to the bathroom, which measured about two feet by two and a half feet – not big enough to keep a small dog in. Her feet were tied together with bandages, her hands tied behind her back with white canvas wrist restraints bought at a medical supply store on Madison Avenue in Orangevale, near where they used to live. Theresa Knorr also removed the knob from the bathroom door and used it on the outside of the cupboard every time she wanted to open it to inspect her daughter. There was no handle inside the cupboard, so Sheila could not get out. Theresa Knorr told her daughter she would not feed her anything, even water, until she admitted what she had done.

'She wanted Sheila to confess,' Terry later said. 'That was mother's way. Beat them until they confess.'

Weak from lack of food, stinking from perspiration in that steaming hot prison, Sheila knew there was only one way to survive. She confessed to her mother that, yes, she did have VD and, yes, she did get a cure. None of it was true, but Sheila only cared about one thing – getting out of that awful cupboard.

It was agony for Sheila as she crawled out of the tiny space that had been her home for more than a week. Her first taste of freedom was probably as sweet for her as that of any escape from a POW camp.

Theresa Knorr once again switched to her caring, loving mother mode and gently helped her daughter drink some water. Sheila seemed to have made it against all the odds. Even the other children were surprised she had actually got out of the cupboard alive.

But Theresa Knorr was feeding her starving daughter water for an ulterior motive. She asked her what kind of drugs the doctor had given her when he administered the shot that cured her VD.

Sheila stumbled over her reply. That was enough for Theresa. She knew her daughter was lying. Within seconds Sheila was being dragged back to that closet from hell. Her freedom had been so brief. The black hole beckoned ...

'PLEASE! PLEASE LET ME OUT OF HERE!'

The screams and moans coming from that cupboard were constantly heard in the Knorr household. But no one noticed the sounds because Theresa Knorr had insisted on stuffing towels underneath the door to the cupboard to muffle her daughter's cries for help. Only Terry, now fourteen years of age, genuinely seemed to care.

She strained her ears to listen for any telltale signs of her sister's condition inside that small cupboard. A few days after she was locked in there for the second time, Terry heard Sheila rustling around, desperately peeling off her clothes because of the sweltering eighty-five-degree heat that drifted through the day and much of the night.

The third day after Sheila's reincarceration, Terry waited until her mum went out on a rare trip to the local shop before sneaking alongside the cupboard with some refreshment for her stifling, feverish sister. All she could find was two cans of beer.

She held a can to her sister's parched lips because her wrists were still bound behind her back. Sheila was sweating so profusely that her hair was wet through. She asked Terry for water, but at that moment Terry heard the sound of the Ford LTD returning. It was beer or nothing.

Sheila desperately swallowed it; much of the beer dribbled down the side of her mouth as she tried to drink the entire contents of one can in a single gulp. The alcohol might have helped deaden the pain just a little bit …

'There is a light above me. I think it's a hole. I'm gonna climb toward it.'

Those were the last words Terry ever heard her sister Sheila utter. A few moments later she heard a thump, then another, then another … then silence.

Those muffled noises occurred as her sister tried to climb

up the hard pine shelves inside the cupboard. Theresa Knorr had removed the lowest one so she could cram her daughter in there.

Sheila had been using the little ledges that the shelves sat on to hold them up, to climb up in the cupboard towards what she thought was the light of freedom. Those final sounds were the shelves crashing down on that emaciated girl.

For three more days Theresa Knorr and the rest of her clan waited to hear if any more sounds came from the cupboard. They knew that an extended silence probably meant Sheila was dead. On the third day 21 June 1985, Theresa Knorr sent Robert over by bicycle to get his brother Billy Bob from the apartment on Fulton he was sharing with Emily Lewis.

As soon as Billy Bob and Robert got back, Theresa grabbed the bathroom knob, slid it into the lock on the cupboard door and gingerly prised it open. Terry and Billy Bob stood by and looked on.

The awful stench that wafted out of the cupboard was followed by the inevitable proclamation by Theresa Knorr:

'She's dead.'

Lying in that cupboard – barely large enough to store a box of books – was Sheila. Clotted blood was smeared crustily across her cheek. There was a puddle of blood on the floor in front of her face. Her torso was virtually naked. She was curled up in a foetal position with her arms behind her back.

'I can't recall whether her eyes were open or not; but I believe they might have been,' said Terry years later, haunted by the image of her sister's decaying corpse.

Theresa Knorr immediately suggested an outrageous plan to make sure that her daughter's death would never be linked to her family. She told the others she wanted to smash off Sheila's teeth with a hammer so that she could not be identified.

Moments later Theresa had second thoughts. She candidly confessed to the assembled children that even she considered the idea of smashing her own dead daughter's teeth to bits a little daunting.

Theresa then carefully peeled on a pair of yellow Playtex Living Gloves, ripped up a plastic garbage bag and used it to line the cardboard popcorn-cup box Billy Bob had brought home from his work at the nearby Century 21 cinema on Howe Avenue. Theresa used that particular brand of gloves because they had a little diamond-shaped grip on them that obliterated all fingerprints.

Then Theresa sat on her bed with a stack of pink-and-blue-flowered pillowcases and slowly plucked all the hairs off those cases until there were none. She wanted to ensure her family had no connection to the body.

She then took the same pillowcases and lined the garbage bag inside the box with them to soak up any blood. Terry was then ordered to stand outside the house to make sure that nobody was nearby.

Inside, Billy Bob and Robert leaned into that tiny cupboard to pull their sister's remains out into the hallway. But the body would not move because half of the left side of Sheila's face was stuck to the floor where she had been frozen in death.

Billy Bob then decided to remove the door of the closet in order to get more access to take out the body. A few minutes later, having taken the door off, the brothers pulled at the rotting corpse and finally hauled it out.

The boys then put their sister's remains in the box – which had been so carefully prepared by Theresa Knorr – before wrapping silver duct tape around it. Then they carried the box outside and put Sheila in the boot of their mother's Ford LTD. Next they packed shovels in the boot. Robert got in the rear seat in the exact same spot where he sat when they took Suesan off to the mountains almost a year earlier.

Moments later Terry watched as her mum and two brothers drove off into the darkness to find a final resting place for Sheila.

This time Theresa made the long drive up Interstate 80 to the Highway 89 turnoff, but, instead of driving to Squaw Valley where Suesan had been burned, they found a new location near the runway at Truckee Airport.

NINE

'The battered child syndrome ... characterizes
a clinical condition in children who have received
serious physical abuse, generally from a parent
or foster parent.'

PAEDIATRICIAN C. HENRY KEMPE, WHO INVENTED THE TERM
'BATTERED CHILD SYNDROME'

It was hardly surprising that Terry Knorr found herself
choking back the urge to vomit as she started cleaning
out that cupboard of death while her mother and brothers
were out dumping Sheila's body in the mountains.

When they did eventually arrive home, her brother
Robert cut the dismantled closet door up with a saw and
then threw it in the Dumpster at the end of the driveway to
the apartment complex that was attached to the house.
Theresa and Billy Bob then collected all Sheila's belongings
and dropped them in the same Dumpster. There was to be no
olive-oil-burning ritual this time.

Terry, gasping against the pungent odour, tried to drink an

iced grape Crush soda as she scrubbed away on her hands and knees inside that tiny closet. But all she could taste was death. She held her nose, swallowed hard and tried not to breathe in the acrid fumes. Terry's brothers later told her they had tried to bury the box containing Sheila, but, as they were digging, somebody had passed nearby and they got scared and drove off, leaving the container sitting in a clump of bushes.

Theresa Knorr had decided not to burn Sheila's body because she did not want it to look in any way similar to Suesan's death.

Terry's memories of her sister Sheila centre around a cowboy hat that had become like a calling card for the pretty teenager.

'It was black velour or velvet and it had a big, like, feather decoration on the front. And she loved that hat. It was a personal belonging, I mean really personal.'

Minutes after returning to the house, Theresa Knorr got rid of that hat, She thought that, as long as any of her daughter's possessions were there, her spirit would still be there to haunt her.

Theresa Knorr also called up Wes Seegmiller, the lawyer who was chasing the insurance company for compensation after Sheila had been knocked down on Auburn Boulevard, and told him, 'Forget it. I want you to drop the case.'

Soon after Sheila's death, Theresa began voicing her hatred towards her daughter-in-law Connie Sanders. She decided Connie's child should be taken away from her because she believed she was a bad mother. In order to do that, she figured she had to get Connie on unfit-parent charges. With no evidence, she somehow became convinced Connie was drugging the baby so she did not have to feed it regularly.

Theresa decided that her youngest daughter, Terry, should become a police informant and help detectives set up Howard and Connie Sanders for a drug deal. First she told Terry to apply for a driver's licence in her dead sister Suesan's name so that she could appear to be eighteen years old rather than fifteen. Then Terry could be recruited to make what police call a 'controlled buy' of narcotics from her own brother and sister-in-law.

Local narcotics squad detective Richard Lauther had his suspicions right from the start when a mutual contact introduced him to 'Suesan'. The first disastrous drug purchase, in which 'Suesan' was supposed to pick up some amphetamines from Howard Sanders, ended in a no-show. Detective Lauther dropped her a short time later, unaware of the brutality and death that allegedly had occurred inside the Knorr household, but highly suspicious of the young girl's real age.

When the detective had asked Terry about her sisters, she replied coolly, 'One ran off with an Indian to go work in Canada, and my other sister just up and left home one day.'

Terry was already passing into what psychiatrists describe as the denial stage of her horrendous childhood. The Knorrs' neighbour on Bellingham, Sean Martin, met up with Robert Knorr long after the family had moved to the small house just off Auburn Boulevard. Robert, unlike his younger sister, dropped a huge hint about what had happened to one sister, but not the other.

'It was weird,' Martin later said. 'First time I saw him, he said Sheila had met a used-car salesman in Vegas who had swept her off her feet. Then a year later I met him and he told me that Satan worshippers had come back and gotten his sister Suesan and set her on fire just off Highway 89.'

On that second meeting with Sean Martin, Robert seemed to have changed a lot. He was a much more menacing character, and Sean warned his own brother Chris to steer clear of Robert as well. He seemed really strange. Almost dangerous.

One time, Sean actually visited the house just off Auburn Boulevard, but he could not get past the front door.

'I saw Robert in the street on his bike, and he persuaded me to take a spin down there. Well, it was so creepy at that house.

'As I walked up to the front door, I heard the mother beating Terry with a stick and I could hear other screams coming from the back of the house. Suddenly Robert freaked out completely and said I had to leave. "My mum's freaking out" was all he would say. He was a very pale white colour and seemed very shocked and upset.'

After Theresa Knorr's plan to have her daughter-in-law arrested failed, she turned to Terry as the next object of her continuing war against the other women inside her family.

Those same handcuffs were pulled out of the cupboard and used on Terry with alarming regularity following the deaths of her sisters.

Theresa Knorr was consistent, if nothing else. She had always punished the eldest daughter the most, followed by the second eldest and so on. But now there was only Terry left to bear the brunt of her mother's brutal regime.

In one horrendous incident, the 250-pound Knorr jumped up and down on Terry while she was handcuffed underneath an antique oak desk, crushing the young girl's stomach and seriously affected any chance of her ever having a child.

More than a year after Sheila's death – and following countless beatings at the hands of her mother – Terry heard the news that she hoped might just help to break up this incredibly unhappy family unit.

'We're outta here. We're movin' out,' announced Theresa Knorr. 'Terry, I gotta job for you ...'

TEN

'My mum was a criminal genius. She knew
how to do things so she could get away with them.
That's why I got the hell out.'

Terry Groves, in her statement to police

In the dense pre-dawn mist, no one noticed the slight
figure scrambling out of the back window of the small
house just off Auburn Boulevard, the house that had been
home to the Knorrs for the previous three years. The only
noise was the occasional distant purr of a V8 engine on
Interstate 80, a quarter of a mile to the west.

Terry Knorr's heart was beating at a furious rate. The
seconds were ticking away. Terry would later recall how she
had been instructed by her mother to burn their home to
the ground. It was 3.40 a.m. on 29 September 1986.

Just a few hours earlier, Theresa Knorr had set out the
plan in very professional terms. She had concluded that,
even though the cupboard where Sheila died had been

very carefully cleaned and then another piece of board hammered over the top of the bloodstained floor, it still constituted a risk to her liberty. Lysol wouldn't work. Spic and Span would not get it out of the air. Fire had worked before on one of her daughters. Maybe it would work again. Theresa Knorr was worried that whoever moved into the apartment after them would probably rip out that board and see the bloodstains.

She instructed her only surviving daughter to wear gloves, spray Gulf charcoal lighter fluid all around the house quickly, then get out of the window, before throwing the match in and running down the street to the motel where she was sharing a room with Robert.

The scared, confused sixteen-year-old spread the contents of the lighter fluid throughout the house and threw a lighted match on the floor *before* she had got out of the back window – and almost ended up suffering the same fate as her sister Suesan.

Scorching heat brushed the soles of her bare feet as she scrambled out of the window, the flames already licking through the back of the inside of the house.

Not daring to even look behind her, Terry just kept hearing her mother's orders: 'Keep running. Keep running.'

In the distance, sirens wailed.

As she weaved through the trailer park and towards the exit to Auburn Boulevard, Terry saw a fire truck turning in towards the house. But no one stopped her. No one even noticed her.

A few minutes later, out of breath and adrenaline still pumping furiously, Terry banged on the door of the room at the Las Robles Motel on Auburn. Theresa Knorr answered. Robert stood sheepishly in the background.

The fire at the house on the 2400 block of Auburn Boulevard was investigated by Officer Stan Brock. He found some clothes left in a rear bedroom by the Knorrs and rapidly came to the conclusion that there was absolutely no doubt the blaze had been started deliberately.

He also noted in his report on the day after the fire that Theresa 'Knorr Ross Sanders' – it should have been Knorr Cross Sanders – was three months behind with her rent and had been served with an eviction notice.

Case #86-86905 was never solved by the Fire Department, despite the fingers of accusation being pointed so firmly at Theresa Knorr and her clan. They tried to locate the family, but no one seemed to know where they had moved.

Howard Sanders thought he would actually behave like a dutiful son and visit his mother a few days later, so he got quite a shock when he turned up at the house, completely unaware of what had happened.

Stunned by the burned-out shell of the property, he strolled across the street to the property manager's office. But all that earned Howard was a very painful earache.

'You know what happened. Your family set fire to it!' the manager screamed hysterically.

'Well, do you know where they went?'

'No. Good riddance!'

She slammed the door so hard in his face he thought it would come off its hinges.

While no one had any clue as to the grisly killings that had allegedly occurred inside the house, there was a definite feeling in the neighbourhood that Theresa and her brood of children were a strange bunch.

Susan Sullivan, who lived in the apartment block attached to the one-storey house, witnessed firsthand a classic example of Theresa Knorr's cunning a few days after the blaze.

'She came up to my apartment and asked me if I had seen anyone hanging around outside the house, because some of her stuff was missing. I told her the door had been left wide open after the fire, so all sorts of people were coming and going. She seemed really pissed off at me, almost as if she was accusing me of stealing stuff out of there. But, from what I recall, there was nothing worth taking anyhow. It was all burned to a crisp.'

And she added: 'I can't put my finger on it, but they were real weird people. The way they moved around. The way they talked. There was something not quite right about them. I wouldn't have wanted to cross them.'

Fellow neighbour William Hall, who lived on the ground floor of the adjoining apartment block with his wife and young child and had become quite friendly with the Knorrs, has never forgotten that night. The heat was so intense the walls of his apartment were too hot to touch.

He believes he and his family were lucky to escape with their lives.

It wasn't as though Theresa Knorr had a split personality. She appeared to be aware of what she was doing and where she was. According to her surviving children, she did not suffer from blackouts or fits of fury. For Terry, it was a part of her life that she could not understand, except that her mother had exercised such control and power over her family that it appeared to drive her to committing acts of violence. Terry knew that whatever was inside her mother prevented her from truly loving anyone. Theresa Knorr had professed love to her children on many occasions, but she could not possibly have experienced true love. She never asked forgiveness. Terry believed that her only fear was that her precious boys would all eventually abandon her ...

With Howard married and Billy Bob living with a girl on the other side of town, Robert became the apple of his mother's eye. He was the one person in her life whom she could cherish and adore. Yet there had been no strong ties between them when the killings began a few years earlier. Robert was the brother who turned squeamish at the sight of Suesan dying on the kitchen floor. He was also the one who sat terrified in the back of the car with her as she lay close to death en route to her outdoor cremation in the mountains.

Robert also took no direct part in actually pouring the petrol over Suesan. Terry says it was Billy Bob who threw the match on their sister's fuel-soaked body.

After the fire at the house near Auburn Boulevard, Theresa Knorr and Robert stayed at the motel for a few days. Billy Bob was over at the apartment he shared with live-in lover Emily Lewis. Terry, meanwhile, saw the whole sequence of events as a perfect opportunity to escape, and she headed off for the red-light districts where Sheila had worked the streets just eighteen months earlier. Anything was preferable to life with her mother.

Eventually, Robert and his mother headed a couple of miles east to Carmichael, another suburb of Sacramento. It was around this time that Theresa cut her long dark hair and started using a variety of blond wigs, and even sometimes dyed her hair as well. No one knows if her change in appearance was prompted by her own in-built fear of one day being apprehended for the alleged murder of her daughters, or just the simple vanity of an overweight woman reaching middle age.

But a blond and far more expensively dressed version of Theresa Knorr started to be seen out at the shopping malls in the area, usually with tall, handsome Robert dutifully following behind, loaded up with shopping bags.

Daughter-in-law Connie Sanders met Theresa Knorr at her apartment in Carmichael on one occasion. She was astonished by the new blond look. She also noticed that much of Theresa Knorr's anger and hatred seemed to have disappeared.

Theresa Knorr even persuaded Connie – once her sworn enemy – to try on the clothes she had worn when she was younger so she could see them once again. The fashion display by her daughter-in-law appears to have been a rather feeble attempt by a grossly overweight woman to fantasise about what might have been.

A few months later, Robert dropped by at his brother Howard's apartment, saying he wanted to see his niece and nephews. Howard was naturally curious to find out how his mother was keeping. But Robert was mysteriously reticent.

'She's living with a guy,' came the kid brother's reply. But he refused to say who or where.

'Is she planning on getting married to this guy or something?' Howard asked, well aware that his much married mother did not make a habit of living with men unless she intended to marry them.

Robert indicated that her intentions were to remarry, but he continued to refuse to provide any details of who might become Howard's latest stepfather. Then Robert told him that their mother did not want Howard to know where she lived. The conversation ended abruptly, and Howard never saw his brother again.

Sometime later, Robert once again came looking for his older brother, but Howard had been jailed for a year for spousal abuse, so he never even realised his half-stepbrother was trying to find him.

By this time, Terry had already established herself in the same profession her tragic sisters had been involved in – prostitution. A brief reunion with her real father, Robert Knorr Sr., had ended abruptly when he tried to molest her after telling her that she reminded him of her mother Theresa.

Her passport to vice was, ironically, another California driver's licence in the name of her dead sister Suesan Marline Knorr. This time the address given was 5804 Garibaldi Street, Sacramento. Unlike the earlier fraudulent licence issued for Terry's undercover work on behalf of the narcs, this one described her hair as red and her weight as 155 pounds, an apparent increase of twenty-two pounds. At least the date of birth, 9-27-66, was the same.

The licence had the words *Age 21 in 1987* emblazoned across it. But it provided Terry with a safe haven from childcare authorities who might put her in a home if she was picked up by cops and gave her true age at the time – just sixteen years old.

As Terry told detectives years later, 'I got that so I could be with the older crowd and not be caught for being so young. The people I was living with at the time were basically hiding me out from my mother and my family.'

Another licence was eventually applied for by Terry so she could safely continue her work as a prostitute with a lady named 'Debra'. She convinced Terry to reapply for a licence in Suesan's name the moment her sister would have been twenty-one so that she would not have problems going into local bars where many potential customers hung out.

Terry held on to that licence and her sister's identity for another five years, in fear that her family or authorities might trace her.

Back on the mean streets of Sacramento's red-light district, word of Terry's tragic background filtered through to many of the girls working the area. Stories of abuse, sexual molestation and poverty are ten a penny among women and men forced to work in the vice trade. Some of Terry's new friends were particularly interested in adopting the identity of her other dead sister. One girl, known only as Mara, skimmed the details of Sheila's short life from conversations with Terry and got herself a driver's licence in her name. It was years later that police realised the girl named as Sheila Gay Sanders on the licence was in fact a petty criminal.

Terry's career on the streets was heavily influenced by Debra, who supplied her with drugs when she needed them and even owned a boutique in the area.

Debra was not exactly Terry's fairy godmother, but she did at least guide the teenager sufficiently to help her earn enough cash to stay out of her mother's clutches. She also introduced Terry to her lawyer, after Terry had told her about the killings of her two sisters.

Terry desperately wanted to see her mother brought to justice for those horrendous deaths. Up until that point, she simply had not met anyone in authority whom she could trust enough to even consider telling the full story to.

Debra provided her young friend with a Valium to swallow before her interview with the lawyer to calm her nerves.

Terry told the lawyer the entire story, *but absolutely nothing happened*. There was no follow-up by him to her. He made no attempt to contact the police to get them to look into her claims. Terry was bewildered and decided that perhaps it had all been a stupid idea. She slotted those painful incidents back into a fragment of her memory bank and closed the door.

Unfortunately, Debra – who in a bizarre fashion had become almost like the mother Terry needed so desperately – eventually turned nasty on her young friend in just the sort of way Terry had become used to back in the Knorr household. The incident that caused such an acrimonious parting of the ways for the vice girl and her sugar mummy occurred when Terry tried to reverse Debra's car out of a driveway, hit the accelerator instead of the brake and ended up crashing into a passing car. A furious Debra threatened to make Terry work in a notorious whorehouse in Vallejo to pay for the damage. But Terry had no intention of being trapped in a vice den.

Once again it was time for her to run away. Keeping on the move somehow made her life more easy to cope with.

Meanwhile, the lure of the bright lights of Reno just a hundred miles east on Interstate 80 was proving irresistible for Theresa Knorr and her son Robert. With a few thousand dollars left over from the sale of the house on Bellingham five years before, mother and son decided to head to Nevada and the gambling halls of Reno.

With her startling blond hairstyle in place, Theresa thoroughly enjoyed spending hours at the slot machines and card tables that adorn the ground floors of hotels with such exquisite names as the Peppermill and the Nugget. One of her favourite places was Fitzgerald's, a name that would come to haunt her years later when the hand of justice finally caught up with her.

Reno – the next biggest answer to Nevada's multibillion-dollar gambling habit after Las Vegas – is known in some circles as 'life's garbage can' because of the wandering souls of northern and central California who stream into the city from Interstate 80.

Theresa Knorr and Robert quickly put a deposit down on a modest apartment on the 1200 block of West Second Street. But she must have found life as the matriarch to just one child a lot different from raising a brood of six.

Robert, nineteen, did not exactly feel indebted to his mother. Thanks to her, he had witnessed and been forced to take part in two appalling murders. Rather than cramp each other's style, they began living separate lives under the same roof. The control frenzy that seemed such an important part of Theresa Knorr's life was crumbling fast.

The streets of central Reno – with its neon lights and tatty skyscrapers – were a melting pot for young drifters, many of whom had run away from the sort of abusive homes that Robert and his brothers and sisters would have longed to be a part of, compared with the unspeakable horrors that occurred in their household.

Robert thrived unhealthily among the oddballs, and soon became caught up in Reno's lowlife. A charge of vagrancy followed after he was found asleep in a doorway to a shop. A burglary was committed, and police later believed it was to obtain drugs.

Two Reno police officers called on Theresa's apartment looking for Robert one day. She was shaken by their visit. Her son's activities were alerting the authorities to her presence – and she wanted to avoid that at all costs. She got out a map, as do tens of thousands of Americans every day, and looked due east on her favourite Interstate 80. Salt Lake City, Utah, looked like the perfect place for her to start a completely new life ...

Over at the office of Nevada County Sheriff William L. Heafey, detectives investigating the 'Body in the Box' case, as it had become known locally, believed they had a major breakthrough.

Fibres taken from the box appeared to match those of the interior carpet in the cab of long-distance trucker Benjamin Herbert Boyle's vehicle. Boyle, from Potter County, Texas, had just been arrested on suspicion of a series of murders of upwards of ten women. Detectives could not believe their luck after they sent off samples to Texas for examination and got the swift reply every law enforcement officer loves to hear: 'It's your man.'

Boyle told detectives he was also pretty grateful to have the opportunity to get the grisly murder off his chest. He was, as they say, singing like a canary.

In Nevada County the investigation into the 'Body in the Box' case was closed.

It seemed that Theresa Knorr's awful alleged crimes were going to remain undetected. It emerged almost eight years later that the two samples of carpet from the serial-killing trucker's vehicle had actually come from the same place. A dreadful administrative error had somehow confused examiners in Texas into believing they had a sample of material from the cardboard box, when in fact the two pieces came from precisely the same truck.

Years later, one of the Placer County detectives investigating the crimes of Theresa Knorr tactfully described his neighbouring county's error as a little embarrassing.

The biggest tragedy of all was that Theresa Knorr's reign of terror could so easily have been brought to a close much sooner ...

Meanwhile, enquiries into the identity of the other Jane Doe #4873/84 – Suesan Knorr – continued to be made by the Placer County Sheriff's Department. At least that case was still marked open and unsolved.

On 1 July 1987, the FBI Academy at Quantico, Virginia-made famous partly thanks to the fictitious detective work of Agent Clarice Starling, played so convincingly by Jodie Foster in *The Silence of the Lambs* – contacted Investigator Brad Marenger at Placer County's substation at Tahoe City to assure him that the National Center for the Analysis of Violent Crime (NCAVC) and the Violent Criminal Apprehension Program (VICAP) had compared the crime analysis report submitted about Jane Doe #4858/84.

But, replied Quantico Unit Chief Alan E. Burgess, 'No linkages have been detected at this time.' 'Linkages' were what Investigator Marenger so desperately needed. He knew only too well that the chances of solving that particular murder were fading rapidly. It would take a miracle to even manage to identify her.

ELEVEN

'The most important point about a mother, your mother, is that she is your mother for always.'

RACHEL BILLINGTON, AUTHOR

Salt Lake City's first real boom occurred when the famous California Gold Rush of 1849–50 resulted in large groups of emigrants trekking through the Salt Lake Valley en route to California. One hundred and forty years later, Theresa Knorr made her own trek to the city from the opposite direction, having decided to create a completely new life for herself.

The city itself, with its thriving cosmopolitan downtown area consisting of a quaint blend of modern tower blocks and classic, older buildings earned a glowing tribute from *U.S. News & World Report*, which dubbed it 'an economic ace and one of sixteen newly bright stars in the U.S. economic sky'. With a population of 700,000 consisting of a multitude of backgrounds, it was the perfect place for Theresa Knorr to blend into anonymity.

While travelling east to Salt Lake, she passed away the hours planning her new existence: a job, a home, new friends, new surroundings, even a new name – she decided to revert to her maiden name, Cross, and became known as that from the moment she arrived in the city. It must have seemed terribly exciting to Theresa. The horrors she had inflicted back in Sacramento had been firmly slotted into a fragment of her mind she had no intention of reopening.

She even read up on the Mormons who founded Salt Lake City back in 1847 and had thrived ever since. US soldiers were stationed in the area in the 1850s, bringing an immense amount of trade with them. Theresa Cross, as she was now known, was particularly interested in Mormon tradition. She had already decided that, when the time was right, she would convert to the Church – it seemed the obvious thing to do if she were going to be easily and quickly accepted in the community.

Theresa Cross based herself in a modestly priced hotel, near the downtown area, bought herself a copy of the Salt Lake City *Tribune* and the *Deseret News*, and started looking for a job. Her only previous employment had been as an orderly in convalescent hospitals, and she had already decided that looking after old ladies would be the perfect career for her new life. It also meant she would get free accommodation and free food and she would not have to live under the same roof as anyone prettier and younger than her.

Theresa's first job was as a live-in help to seventy-two-year-old Alice Powell, riddled with multiple sclerosis, diabetes and arthritis, and in serious need of twenty-four-hour attention. Alice's three daughters all interviewed Theresa in their sick mother's large, single-storey home at 246 North Fourth East Street, Bountiful, a suburb just a few miles north of Salt Lake City. They immediately decided that Theresa was the perfect person for the job. Her transformation was under way.

Theresa Cross soon discovered that her new employer's family were worth many millions of dollars because Alice's parents, at the turn of the century, had bought vast lots of land in the area and then sold them during an economic boom in the fifties. Rumour had it that Alice was worth well over $4 million alone because her husband had retained some of the property and then cleverly developed his own share of the land before selling it.

Within weeks of Theresa starting her new job, Alice's relatives noticed a real improvement in the old lady's condition. They were particularly impressed by Theresa Cross's patience and good nature – something that none of her own children remembers their mother for.

Alice Powell adored Theresa Cross. Theresa was very good to her and regularly took her on outings in her wheelchair. Theresa appeared to really care for the old lady's well-being, and the Powells were delighted with their new recruit.

Alice's sister-in-law, Fran Cheney, seventy-six, and husband Hal, seventy-eight, lived just a few miles north in another suburb, called Centerville, and took a real shine to Theresa.

The elderly couple spent many evenings at Alice's house in Bountiful talking to their newfound friend about the Mormon Church, to which they both belonged at the time. Theresa told them that she had been brought up a Catholic, but that part of her family was of Jewish descent. They spoke in great detail about the workings of the Bible. Theresa had referred to the Bible frequently when she shrieked excerpts from it at her children back in Sacramento.

Theresa Cross had a large collection of different Bibles and she knew the Old Testament particularly well. She regularly exchanged books with the Cheneys, and they gave her copies of a Christian Jewish newsletter about Orthodox Jews who accepted Christ. Eventually, Theresa Cross even joined the Church of Jesus Christ of Latter-day Saints, better known as the Mormons. Her transformation was complete.

But, even though she went to the trouble of being baptised in the Church, she did not have much spare time to devote to it because she had to take care of Alice twenty-four hours a day.

During one evening with the Cheneys, Theresa gave a rare insight into her own upbringing. It was a story filled with rich detail and emotive visions of a childhood in the countryside. No one actually knows how much of it is fact and how much is fiction. She claimed she enjoyed a very happy life in the Midwest on a farm. She even talked about having owned a horse, and, she told the Cheneys, she was very fond of her father.

But then Theresa's voice lowered to a virtual whisper as she told Fran Cheney how her mother had died in her arms when she was just twelve years old, and she provoked even more sympathy by telling her two elderly companions that her grandmother died in the Holocaust.

But, Theresa Cross told her companions, she cursed God for taking her mother away from her at such an early age. She felt bitter about it and blamed that heartbreak for making her get married at a very young age. A few moments later she divulged her own secret guilt. She told Fran and Hal she felt to blame for her mother's death and that God must have put a curse on her, and she said, 'Don't ever go and die on your children.'

Then Theresa surprised her two friends even further by telling them, 'I speak to my mother regularly through the spirits. Through seances and things like that. I still love her very much. When she died, we burned all her belongings on a fire.'

That was exactly what she did with tragic Suesan Knorr in that desolate countryside where they dumped her body.

Another weird aspect of that conversation with the Cheneys was that Theresa referred to her mother as if she were still alive.

But, despite the obvious emotional turmoil she felt, Theresa Cross was very careful not to reveal the pain and anguish she had caused after she became a wife and a mother. Her conversations with the Cheneys suggest that perhaps she always believed that her mother was to blame for everything.

Theresa's lapses revealed small fragments of her past. Like the time she told Fran and Hal about her cruel husband. She never disclosed which one. She never even admitted she had been married more than once.

But Theresa Cross did tell Fran and Hal she believed her husband was a Satanist.

However, Theresa told her friends, 'I wouldn't want to put anyone through what I suffered. I couldn't tell you the things he made me do.'

Then Theresa simply changed the subject. Fran knew not to pry any further into her background.

One day, Theresa took her sick and elderly patient Alice to Park City, Utah, more than thirty miles away, for a special outing. The Cheneys were most impressed when they heard that Theresa had paid for a three-course lunch for the old lady in the ski resort, with her own money.

Fran and Hal Cheney were concerned that their new friend was overworking herself. During her first eighteen months at Alice's house in Bountiful, Theresa Cross never once took a vacation.

'We were so worried about Theresa. Looking after an old lady is relentless work, and, if you don't take any time off, it wears you down after a while,' said Fran.

In fact, Theresa was saving up her $1600 monthly salary and planning her next move with military precision. She had already bought herself a Dodge in her favourite bright red colour to get around in. Her new life had given her new energy – and a determination to further her career in geriatric care.

In the spring of 1990, Theresa Cross enrolled in a night school at the Holladay Health Care Center, about fifteen miles southeast of Salt Lake City, in an attempt to qualify as a fully trained nurses' aide in general healthcare.

On her first night at the imposing three-storey building in Holladay, she met classmate Keith Bendixen. The sixty-seven-year-old hospital orderly was immediately impressed by Theresa, whom he considered to be a classy lady.

At first Keith – who worked in the day at the same healthcare centre in the Salt Lake Valley where the night school was held – felt too shy to exchange anything more than mere pleasantries with the striking but heavy-looking woman. But at break times from the gruelling eight-hour weekly class, the two would walk to the vending machine down the hallway together, and they gradually started to strike up conversations.

To begin with, Theresa talked virtually nonstop to Keith about geriatric care and told him how she looked after an old lady in Bountiful. She even spun a yarn about having one time lived up near Idaho Falls where she did some nursing.

She never once mentioned Sacramento.

It seemed to Keith as if she was deliberately talking mainly about work so as to avoid any pointed questions about her personal life. But, then, the course was incredibly hard work, and anyone who could work from 4.00 p.m. to midnight at night school had to be very dedicated.

About a month into the course, the classmates all had to work three eight-hour days in the actual care centre as part of the practical side of their training. Theresa impressed everyone with her intelligence and devotion to the job.

She had a long list of duties that had to be carefully checked off, and most of the nurses ordering her around were younger and, in many cases, prettier. Theresa Cross was particularly caring towards a number of old ladies with broken hips who had been moved to the healthcare centre from hospitals where their beds were needed for more urgent cases.

'She would get those old ladies up, get 'em dressed, comb their hair and wash them. Then put them in a wheelchair and take 'em to the dining room. Then she would feed 'em, take 'em out of the dining room, and put 'em back to bed. She also had to toilet 'em at least several times a day, as well as clean their beds and put fresh sheets on,' explained Keith admiringly.

Every week the class of ten was given a progress test. Theresa passed with flying colours each and every time. Keith said she was always immaculately dressed and she talked with a very nice accent.

'In class she was always putting her hand up to answer questions and the teacher was always saying she did real good in everything.'

At the end of the three-month course – which cost just eighty dollars – Theresa sailed through the big end-of-term exam and became fully qualified as a nurses' aide in general healthcare.

A few months after finishing the course, Theresa called Keith Bendixen up and asked him if either he or anyone in his family would like to earn some extra money by relieving her for the occasional day at Alice Powell's home in Bountiful.

Soon he, his wife and daughter Marcella were all taking turns to stand in for Theresa whenever she needed days off. She never explained where she was going.

On one occasion, Keith says he stayed overnight at the house after Theresa came home late from some assignation or other. Keith helped fix the hydraulic lift that was used to get Alice into the bath. But the next day, one of Alice's sisters told Theresa they did not want a man staying overnight in the house. Keith never stayed there again. But he did work at the house at least twenty more times.

Often, Theresa would take Keith and his wife out with her and Alice for a meal at the Seven Seas Japanese restaurant in the shopping mall near the house. Sometimes they would also eat out at the Red Lion Cafe. As usual, Theresa showed great generosity by always treating everyone.

Keith received his wages for helping look after Alice Powell out of the $1600 a month that Theresa was paid. Theresa also shelled out cash for most of the delicious food she prepared at the house, because her housekeeping allowance from Alice's daughters of $250 a month did not cover everything.

Keith loaned her countless books on nursing care, and she loaned him her maths and chemistry books. She also owned dozens of books on the development of certain drugs.

Keith remembers Theresa's cooking as being superb. He

would always say a blessing before each meal, which Theresa seemed impressed by.

'Bless this food and do our bodies good and help us. Amen.'

One time, Theresa told Keith she had been on a trip down to San Diego to see her son. It was a rare reference to her family, and untrue, since she had no son in southern California.

But, even more significantly, Theresa Cross told Keith she had just one other son and he had died in a motorcycle crash. *She did not mention her three daughters.*

Sometimes Keith, his daughter Marcella and Theresa would do some Bible readings together. And at breakfast Theresa would sit buried in her chemistry books once Alice had sat down to eat. She told Keith that she was studying hard in the hope of one day being allowed to enrol for a full four-year nursing course to get an R.N. degree. Theresa Cross was thinking bigtime. Her life had taken on an entirely new dimension.

Once again Theresa talked in fictional terms about her upbringing; this time she claimed she had been raised in places like Kentucky and Tennessee. She admitted she wasn't close to her family but had written to them on occasions. Keith – who had at one time sold cars and real estate in California – was intrigued by his new friend. But there was something about her ... he just could not quite put his finger on it.

In Sacramento, more Knorr family problems were brewing

following a surprise visit to Billy Bob's cosy home in North Highlands, near Sacramento, by wayward brother Robert.

At first Billy Bob was fairly pleased to see his kid brother. It had been at least four years since he and Theresa Knorr had skipped town for Reno, and he'd thought about them both many times.

But, when Robert's brief visit turned into months, Billy Bob started to notice habits of his brother's that he never knew existed. Robert was always out until late, and waking up Billy Bob when he struggled into the apartment in the early hours. And Robert was behaving 'differently' from what he had been like before.

Ultimately, Billy Bob kicked Robert out of the house, and never saw him again.

Billy Bob was very careful not to introduce his brother to his new pretty blond girlfriend DeLois, whom he had met when the two attended a radio broadcasting school in Sacramento. They were already deeply in love and talking about marriage.

TWELVE

'The single most consistent finding regarding
juvenile homicide is that kids who kill, especially
those who kill family members, generally have
witnessed or have been directly victimized by
domestic violence.'

CHARLES PATRICK EWING, AUTHOR

When bartender Robert Ward walked into work for
the night shift at Red's Place on North Nellis Boulevard, in Las Vegas, on 7 November 1991, he could not have
had any idea that he was about to become the next victim of
the Knorr family's sick and twisted household.

For Robert Knorr, life in Vegas had become a game of
desperate stakes since arriving from Reno. He had no money
and was living on the streets or scrounging a bed for the
night from some passing stranger. Reno might have been the
garbage can of northern and central California, but Vegas
seemed to be the waste-disposal unit for the entire country.

And Robert's earlier split with his mum when they were
both up in Reno was probably the final straw as far as his

own sense of self-preservation was concerned. Ironically, while he may well have been desperate to get away from her, she did in many ways protect him from himself. How could a man barely out of his teens have any sense of moral purpose in life after experiencing and, his sister Terry claims, taking part in the killing of his two sisters?

Throughout his short life, Robert Knorr had demonstrated an escalating propensity towards violence, a significant trait in an emerging murderer. As a child he had witnessed such horrors that he later admitted he had no real control over his temper. In some ways, he was just asking for the intervention of the criminal justice system. He barely recognised society's laws because punishment had no real meaning to him – he had just been through a childhood that no human being should ever have to endure.

By the time Robert Knorr found himself hanging around outside Red's Place that warm evening, casing the joint and planning an armed hold-up, he had all but given up on life as we know it.

Ten minutes later, bartender Robert Ward was dead after Knorr held him up with a pistol in yet another desperate attempt to feed his drug habit. The police picked Knorr up without a struggle a couple of blocks from the bar a few minutes later.

Intriguingly, Robert Knorr did not even bother to ask for a lawyer when police took him down to the local precinct to be booked and thrown in a holding cell. His only request was for them to get in touch with his mother. He gave them an address. But, when detectives contacted Theresa Knorr, she never returned their calls. The son who must have been turned into a killer by those awful scenes at that little house off Auburn Boulevard was being snubbed by the very person who created his downfall.

Las Vegas Police pressed for first-degree murder charges and, with it, the potential of a cell on Nevada's death row. But in the end they reduced the charge to second-degree murder in exchange for his admission of guilt.

On 25June 1993, he stood before the Eighth Judicial District Court in Las Vegas and was sentenced to sixteen years. His mother never did bother to contact him.

But Robert's problems were of no concern to Theresa Cross, as she was now known. In Salt Lake City, she did not even acknowledge the existence of a son in Las Vegas. She had a new life, after all.

However, there was a slight hiccup to her plans when she took a one-month vacation from her job at Alice Powell's place in Bountiful and ended up staying away for eight weeks. Once again she used that now familiar tale of going to visit her son in San Diego. No one knows where she really went.

Not surprisingly, Alice's daughters decided that they needed someone a little more reliable in charge of their mother, and Theresa was dismissed for taking the extra time off without permission. (Alice's daughters insist to this day that she walked out on the job.)

Ann Cristofersen, fifty-six, took over from Theresa at the

Powell house in Bountiful, and she completely discounts reports of her predecessor's diligence.

'I believe that she left Alice alone on many occasions. Neighbours have told me they would often call around and discover that Theresa was out and Alice was here by herself.'

However, Ann Cristofersen made much more serious allegations about Theresa Cross's treatment of Alice Powell, who is basically unable to attend to anything for herself.

'I think she was sometimes physical with Alice. I have no doubt that she slapped her a few times and used to leave her on the toilet for hours. When I arrived here, I had to spend months getting Alice's confidence because she was so scared every time she had to be taken to the toilet.'

If Ann Cristofersen's claims have any real substance, they completely contradict the opinion of many others in Salt Lake City.

But Theresa's falling out with the Powell family had no effect whatsoever on her friendship with Fran and Hal Cheney over at Centerville. In fact, the elderly couple took pity on Theresa when they heard she was no longer working for Fran's sister-in-law and offered to let her stay in their house while they were away on a trip to Russia in 1992.

Theresa kept the red-brick, detached two-storey house built in the 1920s spotless, watered all the plants and behaved like the perfect guest while they were on their travels. For Theresa Cross, the Cheneys' hospitality would remain indented on her conscience. She never forgot their kindness.

But for the time being she needed to find another job as a

home help to an elderly person. Once again she picked up the local newspaper, the *Deseret News*, and studied the jobs columns in the classified section.

Less than ten miles away from where Theresa Knorr was reading that newspaper, her wayward daughter, the only surviving female child in the Knorr family household, was getting married to the man she hoped would help wipe out those awful memories forever.

In an extraordinary twist of fate, both mother and daughter had ended up running away to the same city. Incredible though it may seem, neither of them apparently had any clue as to the other's whereabouts.

Terry had escaped from the evil clutches of vice girl Debra and then another even more unpleasant madam in Sacramento, when she met and fell in love with softly spoken, hardworking Mike Groves.

He had proclaimed his love for Terry virtually from the moment he clapped eyes on her in a bar, and the two had decided to elope back to Mike's home in Salt Lake City to get married, settle down and live happily ever after. But fairy tales never come true ... especially if you come from a family like the Knorrs.

Terry had so many reasons to want to leave those streets of Sacramento: her mother's abuse, the murders of her two sisters, the sexual molestation, the prostitution, the drugs. Anywhere had to be better than Sacramento as far as she was concerned.

So, when she and Mike travelled up to Salt Lake City, Terry – just like her mum had done a couple of years earlier – saw the streets of this thriving city paved with the sort of happiness she had never experienced in her entire life.

The marriage ceremony was a modest affair held at Mike's parents' house in Sandy, a suburb eight miles southeast of Salt Lake City.

Matron of honour Heidi Sorenson, who went on to become Terry's best friend, explained, 'It was a small, friendly gathering. A simple champagne toast after the ceremony. But I remember that Terry seemed so genuinely happy to be getting married. It was as if she had at last found some true happiness.'

The couple could not afford a honeymoon, but that did not matter to Terry. She had Mike and a new life – that was all that mattered.

But, within months of marrying Mike Groves, all that pain and anguish was to return. The main problem up in Salt Lake City was that she was sharing her in-laws' huge, badly maintained house, in the relatively wealthy suburb of Sandy. And, besides being home to Ma and Pa, there was also Mike's big, slow-witted brother to contend with. The house was dark, gloomy, filled with cheap, broken, outdated furnishings and with a filthy carpet on the floor. The Groves had bought it more than thirty years earlier, and a local housing boom had turned the once deserted area into an upper-middle-class neighbourhood.

The parents tried hard initially. They made sure that Terry

and Mike got some privacy in their basement apartment attached to the main house only by a spiral staircase into the ground-floor hallway. But what Terry did not realise until she got to Sandy was that everyone in the house drank. Soon, domestic arguments were commonplace and, although not on anything like the scale of Sacramento, they had the effect of reminding Terry over and over again of her horrendous childhood.

However much she tried, she could not stop herself from getting drawn into these increasingly violent rows between Ma, Pa and Mike. She had to act to stop the arguments before something dreadful happened. Subconsciously, she felt partly to blame. She felt she was the catalyst for yet more domestic upheaval. Eventually it got to her. She had a fight with Mike, hit him and the police charged her with assault.

Terry soon became a familiar face at the Salt Lake County Jail, where she would spend many nights cooling off after yet another flare-up at home. Terry got quite aggressive inside prison and was known to certain prison officers as a hot-tempered troublemaker.

Sandy Police Department patrolman David Lundberg rolled up to the house in his all-white SPD Taurus one time in 1991. Although police did not arrest anyone on that occasion, Lundberg vividly recalled the house because it was such a high-income home maintained at a low income.

He recalled, 'They were all fighting like cats and dogs. I tried to defuse the situation as best I could, but it all seemed so dysfunctional. In the end we settled things down, but it was pretty obvious there would continue to be problems there.'

David Lundberg never forgot his visit to the house in Sandy, and it would stand him in very good stead one day a couple of years later.

Still only in her early twenties, Terry's desperate search for a happy life had seemingly ground to a complete halt. She loved her husband very much, but she feared that her mother's evil ways were manifesting themselves inside her now. Wed at a young age. No money. Constant rowing. Her married life was turning into a mirror image of the woman whom she so hated and despised.

If Terry had realised that her own mother – the very woman whom she claims caused all her problems – was living a relatively charmed existence just a few miles away, would it have made any difference? As it was, Terry's difficult marriage incited her to try once again to do something to bring her mother to justice. She believed that the only way to finally destroy Theresa Knorr's appalling influence was to get someone to believe her incredible story of life inside that horrendous family.

For the next few months she desperately tried to find someone to tell her story to. First she told a friend, Rhonda Morris, who sat and listened intently to Terry but then decided to ignore her extraordinary claims because she thought Terry had said her mother was already in jail for the killings.

Terry went on to inform at least five other individuals

about the murders, including a psychiatrist in Salt Lake City, two employees at the Valley Mental Health Clinic, and even a mental-health counsellor she encountered during one of her spells inside the Salt Lake County Jail.

But no one seemed concerned enough to go to the police themselves. Many of them could not accept or believe Terry's story of mental, physical and sexual torture.

Meanwhile, the domestic crisis inside her in-laws' house in Sandy continued. When would someone stand up and take notice of what she was saying?

THIRTEEN

'The vast majority of abused children treat
their parents much better than their parents
have ever treated them.'

PAUL MONES, *WHEN A CHILD KILLS*

Terry felt an icy chill run through her body. She shivered
and looked up. It was pitch-black, except for a tiny sliver
of light in the corner above her. Instinctively, she pushed the
palm of her hand upwards. It smacked against something
cold and plastic. She pushed hard again, this time with both
hands. She had to get to that light. It was her only chance.
But the ceiling would not move. The only noise was the crisp
crumpling of the frozen bags that lined the floor she was
lying on. As she adjusted her position, her elbow brushed
the side of the wall next to her. It gave off a slight burning
sensation because of the sub-zero temperatures. Terry was
trapped in a deep freezer.

Sitting on the door to the coffin-shaped freezer was her

250-pound mother. She was punishing her youngest daughter because she thought Terry had been saying bad things about her to her teacher at school.

Inside the freezer, Terry gasped for air. Clouds of icy steam surrounded her every breath. She looked up at that small crack of light once again.

'There's a light above me. I think it's a hole. I'm gonna climb toward it.'

'There's a light above me. I think it's a hole. I'm gonna climb toward it.''

Terry's sister's voice just would not stop repeating the words over and over again.

Just then a movement from above. The door opened. The bulky shape of her huge mother was silhouetted against the light. Unlike her tragic sister Sheila, Terry had made it to that light above.

Terry awoke from her nightmare relieved to find that this time it had all been a fantasy. The freezer incident had been yet another appalling act committed against her by her mother a few years earlier. Her dreadful dreams had haunted her for more years than she cared to remember and they left her feeling angry, confused, even betrayed. Her anger was because her mother had disappeared into thin air and allegedly got away with murder. She felt confused because Theresa Knorr's liberty implied that it was OK for parents to abuse and hate children – maybe they all did that? But the worst aspect was the betrayal that Terry felt because none of the people she told about her terrible childhood experiences had done anything to help bring Theresa Knorr to justice.

Only a few days earlier, Alan Rice, a counsellor at the Valley Mental Health Center in Salt Lake City, had pleaded with Terry to go and tell the police one last time after he listened with horror to her story. But no one understood that Terry was afraid of walking into a police station alone and retelling her story. In any case, it had got to the point where she wondered if it was worth it.

But that evening – with Alan Rice's advice still ringing in her ears – Terry decided to pour out her innermost secrets to Heidi Sorenson, her best friend in Salt Lake City. They had become very good friends after Terry married Mike Groves, who just happened to be the best friend of Heidi's then-husband. Heidi was the matron of honor at the wedding ceremony held at Terry's in-laws' house in Sandy. Terry would often drive over to Heidi's place in her little truck, where she would sit and chat with her friend and maybe cook up a little pasta.

Heidi, now twenty-six, explained, 'Terry seemed to be very introverted. Into herself. I remember when I first met her she was very difficult to get to know. She is a jeans and T-shirt type of person and comes across as kinda hard-core because of what she has been through.'

Heidi and Terry were sitting around at Heidi's neat duplex home in Woods Cross, yet another Salt Lake City suburb, on 26 June 1990, when Terry told her friend she had something on her mind.

'I've got these things that are really bothering me. D'you mind if I tell you 'bout them?' asked Terry hesitantly.

She was close to giving up on ever getting her mother brought to justice, but she felt the urge to have a sounding board, a shoulder to cry on, and Heidi seemed the only true, genuine friend she had.

Heidi had absolutely no clue what Terry was about to tell her. Terry had never even told her husband the full details of those horrendous years in the Knorr household, and it was hardly something you talked about over popcorn at the movies or dinner at Denny's, which were the sorts of things the two couples had done together.

Tears welled up in Terry's eyes before she had even begun to tell her friend. Heidi's two young children were still up, but playing so noisily in the kitchen that they would never have overheard the disturbing story Terry was about to reveal.

She told Heidi everything: the killings of her sisters, the beatings and torture she received, the abuse inflicted to and by her brothers, her sister's mottled hair when they found her body rotting in that cupboard, Suesan's desperate cries for help.

Terry then lowered her voice to a whisper.

'Sometimes I think I am going crazy. I wonder if I imagined it all. No one ever seems to believe me.'

Heidi was so stunned by her friend's account of life as a child that for a few moments she also wondered if Terry was actually telling the truth.

'It was so bizarre. It was hard to believe things like that could have happened,' says Heidi now. Then she felt a chill in the air, thinking about what her friend had just told her. 'The house seemed to get real cold after she told me. It was weird. Almost as if ...'

Heidi put her arm around Terry, who sobbed, 'I can't understand why nothing has been done. I can't understand.'

Heidi was appalled by what Terry told her. 'It just wasn't right that someone could get away with doing those things,' she said.

Terry had so much bottled up inside her, but she felt she could trust Heidi. She told her friend about the never-ending nightmares and how what had happened had stopped her from getting into many relationships. How it had affected her schoolwork; she did not even graduate from school.

Heidi particularly remembered that because the two women were, in many ways, like chalk and cheese. She had been to college and was even studying nights at business school to get more knowledge of the legal aspects of big businesses.

It was around 9.00 p.m. by the time a tearful Terry finished telling her horror story. Heidi, appalled by what she had heard, felt she had to help in some way. Then she remembered that her sister used to go out with the son of the local sheriff. He would do something, she thought. But, when Heidi told Terry that she was going to call Sheriff Clarence Montgomery of the Woods Cross Sheriff's Department immediately, Terry was not overly impressed. After all, she had already told a number of people she thought were in authority, and they had done absolutely nothing.

But this is a cop, Heidi assured her. Not some fancy psychiatrist or social worker. This was someone out on the streets who would actually know how to get some action. She picked up the phone.

'I got someone here you gotta talk to, Sheriff. I need you to come over tonight ...'

The moment Heidi mentioned the word 'murder', Montgomery's ears pricked up. Woods Cross, a suburb with a population of just 6,000, ten miles north of Salt Lake City, had seen only one murder in more than thirty years.

'I'll be right over.'

By 11.00 p.m. Sheriff Clarence Montgomery was sitting down on Heidi's couch, his Sony Dictaphone minicassette recorder whirling as he prepared to listen to the most extraordinary account of domestic abuse he would ever hear, even in his long and distinguished career.

With the kids now safely tucked up in bed, a deathly, expectant silence shrouded the house. Sheriff Montgomery asked red-eyed young Terry sitting opposite him to run through the whole story one more time.

Terry started from the beginning once again. Maybe this time something would actually get done. Heidi sat next to her friend, holding her hand for comfort.

Heidi was surprised to notice Sheriff Montgomery's attention wavering several times as Terry told her account of life back in Sacramento. In fact, he dozed off several times. But it was very late at night.

At around 12.30 a.m. the minicassette clicked off as it

came to the end of the second side of the tape and that marked the end of the interview. Unfortunately, the batteries in the machine were too low to record the latter half of the interview, it was later revealed by embarrassed investigators. Heidi did not dare tell Terry that she was a little concerned about the sheriff's catnapping. She just hoped that something would now be done to track down Theresa Knorr.

Terry went to great efforts to emphasise to the sheriff that she had told many others, who had done nothing, and she hoped some action would be taken. The sheriff assured her that it would.

Next day, Montgomery carefully wrote up a report of his visit to Heidi Sorenson's home. Then a letter from Woods Cross Chief of Police Paul Howard was enclosed with Montgomery's report, plus the tapes of the interview, and dispatched to the Sacramento Police Department's Homicide Division Commander.

The letter read:

Dear Investigator,

Theresa Knorr Groves of 2020 E. Pepperwood Drive, Sandy, Utah, contacted one of our officers and related some information concerning a possible homicide that occurred in 1982 and a second homicide that occurred in 1985 or 1986 in your area.

Theresa Groves, DOB 8/5/70, stated that she was raised in the Sacramento area and lived with her mother, Theresa J. Knorr, possible date of birth 3/14/ 46. Her maiden name was Theresa Cross, but she has used the names of Boyington, Sanders, Harris, Knorr, and Cross. She has worked as a nurse.

She lists the children as Howard, DOB 7/16/63; Sheila, DOB 3/13/65; Susan [sic], DOB 9/27/66; William, DOB 9/17/67; Robert, DOB 12/31/68; and herself.

She says that her mother tortured and shot Susan [sic], and then disposed of her body in a car fire after several months. This occurred in 1982.

Her mother also killed Sheila by physically abusing her, keeping her tied up in a closet, and after she died the body was disposed of by a car fire near Truckee.

Her mother had also shot her first husband but had been acquitted of that homicide.

These incidents occurred at 2410 Ivory Boulevard, Apt. #A, but the apartment had been burned down to cover up the evidence of Sheila's death.

Being fearful for her life, Theresa left the Sacramento area and has been in the Salt Lake area since 1988. She has recently been arrested for intoxication and has used drugs in the past and is currently seeing an Alan Rice at the Valley Mental Health Center in Salt Lake. She told him about this information and he advised her to give the same information to the police.

She is currently living within the jurisdiction of the Sandy City, Utah, Police Department and was only in our area to visit a friend at the time she contacted our officer.

I have run the names NCIC with negative results on any of them.

Our officer did record the majority of the conversation, however, without his realizing it, the batteries went dead and the entire conversation was not recorded. I have enclosed the tape for your use.

If we can be of any further assistance, please contact me.

Sincerely,

Paul Howard Chief of Police

In Sacramento, Howard's letter, Montgomery's report and the tape – sealed in a registered envelope – were received by Lt. Ken Walker, head of the homicide detail. He assigned a detective to look into the allegations. That detective checked out the details and promptly proclaimed the allegations an unlikely tale after failing to link any homicides with Terry's claims about the deaths of her sisters.

While there certainly are a number of errors in the letter, the basic essence of what had occurred is clearly and accurately stated.

Terry's phone number is at the beginning of the letter, yet no one from Sacramento ever called her. Unfortunately, as it later emerged, the police only contacted officials in Nevada County, where the body of Sheila had been incorrectly linked to the killings committed by Texan truck driver Benjamin Herbert Boyle. Sacramento detectives never contacted the Placer County Sheriff's Department, where Suesan's charred remains were discovered, and her murder continued to be unsolved. Years later, as questions flew around the Sacramento police headquarters, officials noted that Terry had, in her statement to Montgomery, mentioned Truckee as the location where Suesan's body was burned, and they presumed that to be in the Nevada County jurisdiction.

When the calls from Woods Cross Sheriff's Department stopped coming in after those first few weeks of activity, Terry assumed that yet again her pleas for justice had gone unnoticed. Perhaps it would be better to stop retelling those horror stories and get on with her life, she thought to herself. But the nightmares just would not let her forget.

Heidi and Terry never mentioned it ever again. In fact, the two friends lost touch when Heidi's marriage fell apart and Terry's seemed under severe stress.

Heidi is still astonished by the lack of a police investigation following Sheriff Montgomery's visit to her home that night.

Those vivid images of child abuse retold so chillingly by Terry haunted her friend Heidi for years. It got so bad at one stage that she could not bring herself to go out to the storage shed in her backyard because it reminded her of the cupboard where Sheila had perished. Heidi could even imagine the smell of rotting flesh inside that cupboard, thanks to an incident years earlier when she found herself standing near a corpse in a hospital elevator.

'There was no light in there and I remember getting goose bumps when I went in it. I couldn't stop thinking about what happened,' recalled Heidi.

Just ten miles south of Woods Cross, Theresa Cross, as she now called herself, was blissfully unaware of just how close she had come to being arrested. Her main priority at that time was finding a new job following her departure from Alice Powell's house in Bountiful.

As she carefully studied the classified section of the *Deseret News*, an advertisement caught her eye.

Care Giver for elderly lady. Full time salary plus room and board. Please phone …

A few hours after calling the number, Theresa Cross – the one-time alleged mom from hell turned saintly nurse to the sick and elderly – was handing over two sparkling references to retired bank executive Bud Sullivan and his sister Pat Thatcher, who were interviewing her for the job of care giver to their elderly mother, Alice Sullivan.

Bud Sullivan was impressed by her knowledge of medications. Pat, whose husband Vere was a retired Salt Lake City detective, was just as enthusiastic.

Theresa Cross was particularly proud of her certificate from the state government that proclaimed her to be a fully qualified healthcare worker. She even gave Bud Sullivan the number of her certificate just in case he wanted to check it out.

'I figured that, since she gave me the number, it had to be true,' remembered Bud.

By the time Theresa Cross had left Bud's mum's home in east Salt Lake City where the interview was conducted, both he and his sister were convinced she was the perfect person for the job.

Bud had actually hired another woman a few days earlier, but she had not even showed up for her first day of work at the Sullivan house.

'Theresa seemed so solid in comparison. We both knew she was the right one for the job,' said Bud.

FOURTEEN

'The emotional development of children is
intimately connected to the safety and nurture
provided by their environment.'
BESSEL VAN DER KOLK, HARVARD MEDICAL SCHOOL PSYCHIATRIST

By December of 1992, Theresa Cross was lapping up
her new life in Salt Lake City with relish. All those
memories of what happened back in Sacramento had been
neatly filed away. She was now the loving, caring nurse to
elderly Alice Sullivan, and the added bonus was Alice's
family, who all readily accepted Theresa Cross into their lives
and homes. Later, they used words like 'good' and 'kind' to
describe the woman whom her daughter Terry knew as
one of the most cold-blooded mothers in criminal history.

'Theresa was a great person. My mother just loved her.
Everybody in the family loved her,' recalled Bud Sullivan,
Alice's son.

That affection towards Theresa Cross came to a pleasant

head at Christmastime that year. Bud and his sister Pat insisted that she be involved in every aspect of the yuletide festivities. The contrast between the punishments she inflicted so horrifically on her children that most of them have blocked Christmas out of their minds completely, and life in Salt Lake City that year could not be greater.

Christmas Eve at Alice Sullivan's neat single-storey corner house on 1504 South 600 East was, according to family tradition, when the presents were handed out among twenty-five of the closest family members.

Over the years, Bud Sullivan – with all his years' experience as an executive at the First Interstate Bank, Utah – had devised a sensible system so that no one in the family had to buy gifts for everyone because that would be ludicrously expensive. Instead, the entire family wrote their names on a piece of paper and dropped it into a hat and drew just one name out at a time, so that no one had to purchase more than one present. Naturally, Theresa was included in that.

She sat with the four generations of Sullivans around Alice's vast Christmas tree, bedecked with lights and decorations, and savoured every moment. Who knows if she even once considered the plight of her surviving children scattered around the country, suffering endless nightmares of the dreadful injuries she allegedly inflicted on them?

On Christmas Day itself, the Sullivans reconvened back at Alice's house for Christmas dinner. Theresa Cross could not believe her luck. The holiday celebrations were continuing, and the family had insisted she stay involved throughout.

Dinner that day consisted of a huge turkey cooked to perfection at Alice's daughter Pat's home just around the corner. Everything else – salads, turkey dressing, apple and pumpkin pies, all the vegetables – were prepared by Theresa Cross in Alice's kitchen. Her own children recalled that mealtimes at home in Sacramento usually consisted of microwave fast food ... if they were lucky.

The Christmas celebrations that day were rounded off with a bourbon toast for all the adults, including Theresa. Bud Sullivan was impressed that the warm and caring lady looking after his mother only drank alcohol very occasionally. And she had to be forced to accept a drink that day. Bud was surprised that Theresa Cross did not seem to want to say too much about her past, especially her children. But he figured he shouldn't pry, so he never pressed her on the subject.

Bud's sister Pat Thatcher had a little more intuition, and tried to pump Theresa Cross for further information. But Theresa was very evasive. She did tell Pat she had no daughters, and talked in hushed tones about how she had two sons, but one had been killed in an accident. It was a fantasy, but, as with the Cheneys back in Bountiful, how could anyone know she was lying?

Pat had the overriding impression that Theresa Cross was a very private kind of person who made everyone feel they shouldn't ask too many questions. The only background about Theresa's upbringing came in a brief reference to being brought up on a farm in Iowa. But it was a fleeting comment that she never expanded upon. Theresa did confide in Pat that she was happy to be working for them and considered them to be her adopted family.

Bud and Pat were eternally grateful to have discovered Theresa. She seemed a real gem. Not many people would work around the clock without a word of complaint. It was almost as if Theresa was punishing herself by being so solid and reliable.

Her typical day at Alice Sullivan's house started at 5.00 a.m., when she liked to get up and get things done about the house before Alice woke up. Often she would pop out to do some errands in the morning and let Alice sleep in – unlike her previous charge, Alice Powell, this Alice was fairly active and compos mentis: On returning from her errands, it would be time for her to get Alice up, bathe her and give her breakfast. However, Theresa spent a lot of time reading in her room in the middle of the day. Both Bud and Pat would often ring the front door of the house and have to wait some moments before Theresa waddled through the house to open up. Alice, usually sitting in her favourite chair near the front window, was not expected to start answering doorbells.

Pat Thatcher's only concern about Theresa was that she never seemed to want to take any time off. Theresa happily took Alice Sullivan to the Our Lady of Lourdes Catholic Church, on the corner of Eleventh East and Seventh South

146

most Sundays, and she was very conscientious about making sure the old lady – who was eighty-six at the time – got whatever she required.

'Theresa would often call me up and say, "Your mother needs this and that." I would say, "Fine, Theresa, you go get it and give me the bill and I'll pay you,"' says Pat.

But her mother's nurse often did not give Pat the bill – preferring instead to pay for the old lady herself. Frequently, Theresa would spring for a blouse or a pair of shoes for Alice – all paid for with her own hard-earned cash. She made a special effort to make Alice look nice whenever they both ventured out.

On Valentine's Day –14 February 1993 – she even bought Alice a gift to celebrate. Pat, meanwhile, kept saying to herself, 'This lady is too good to be true …'

Bud Sullivan did find it strange that Theresa Cross spent so much time in her little bedroom at the back of the house, even though she had the run of the place. But he reckoned it was none of his business, so he did not mention it to Theresa.

That nine-by-nine room at the back of the Sullivan house became a virtual shrine to Theresa Cross. It was filled with jewellery and a wardrobe crammed with expensive clothes. That room was the one place she could gather her real thoughts and fears … and face the memories of the past. The room itself was always kept immaculately clean. A bedspread coloured dark blue, with streaks of blood red, adorned the queen-size bed that was provided by the Sullivans, although Theresa insisted on buying herself a new mattress. Matching drapes were closed for much of the time against the light. Just like back in Sacramento, there were no pictures on the wall, no evidence of family or friends. But on a white cabinet lay a vast range of expensive make-up: Christian Dior, Lancôme, and other designer labels. Under the bed was a box filled with receipts from restaurants, shops, and hotels that she had collected during her travels over the previous few years. The bills were from as far afield as East Illinois and California. In another box under the bed, yet more make-up. In one corner, there was a large maple double dresser with a full-length mirror in which she would constantly check her appearance. Inside the dresser, there were many pairs of shoes, nearly all a safe, one-inch heel. Theresa had so many clothes that Bud had to build her an overspill rail on the enclosed porch outside the back of the house.

Many of her dresses, skirts, and trousers were red. Red was her favourite colour. It tended to be a very crimson shade of red. The colour of blood.

Dozens of books lined the shelf of the white cabinet. They included books on Jews, Catholics and Mormons. There were also many on the development of new drugs, plus one on herbal medicine. She also had medical manuals that described how to deal with people with Parkinson's and Alzheimer's diseases. Theresa's pride and joy was her own phone line. She had paid almost a hundred dollars to have it installed within days of taking the job at Alice Sullivan's. Sometimes she would spend hours making secretive phone calls in her room.

But, much more surprising, in her double dresser there were at least six wigs. Blond, brunette, red, all lengths and shapes.

The neat, dark-haired bob hairpiece looked just like the hairstyle she had in her Utah driver's licence photo. Neither Pat nor Bud ever recalls seeing Theresa Cross wearing any of the wigs. No one has any idea why she kept them.

Theresa Cross's errands were usually carried out before Alice Sullivan woke up, and often included a trip to her local Albertson's Supermarket to stock up on food for the house. No one knows if she ever noticed the girl at the checkout or if that girl recognised her. For Theresa Knorr's daughter Terry worked at that same Albertson's for most of the first half of 1993.

'They could even have glanced at each other – who knows?' reckoned one of the detectives who interviewed Terry later.

Terry even told investigators, 'I felt the presence of my mother nearby. I knew she was close.'

Whatever the implications of Terry's 'sixth sense' about her mother's close proximity, there were a number of other strange incidents that occurred around this time:

1. Bud Sullivan and his sister Pat Thatcher say that Theresa Cross became much more secretive and reclusive around the beginning of 1993. She also seemed to be spending all her weekly wages, even though she had virtually no living expenses and, according to Bud, must have been capable of saving at least $1000 to $1200 a month.

Bud's brother-in-law, Vere Thatcher – the former Salt Lake City Police detective – later speculated that Theresa Cross may have been blackmailed.

2. Why did Howard Sanders suddenly decide to track down his long-lost half-brother Billy Bob after more than five years apart? Eventually Howard's new fiancée traced Billy in June 1992, and the two half-brothers met up to discuss what to do about their mother. But William Knorr wanted to just forget the past, according to statements later made to detectives.

3. Howard told the Placer County investigators that he kept in touch with his only surviving half-sister, Terry Knorr, through a lawyer called Carl Swain, who is also currently representing Howard's new fiancée in a personal-injury suit. How much influence did this have on bringing Theresa Cross to justice, and what messages were passed between the two?

4. According to Howard, Terry called her brother Billy Bob's wife, DeLois, on a number of occasions. These phone calls have been described in police testimony by Howard Sanders as being 'threatening'. DeLois refused to put her husband Billy Bob on the phone to his sister, and told Terry, 'No, you're not getting any money out of Bill. You tell me why you want to get ahold of him?' During the call, Terry just kept repeating: 'Let me talk to Bill. Let me talk to Bill.'

DeLois later contradicted what Howard had claimed by telling investigators that Terry had called up, but she had pretended to Terry that she had rung up the wrong William Knorr.

5. Why did Robert Knorr Sr. and his son Billy suddenly reunite around this same time, even though they had not been in touch for sixteen years? Billy insisted to investigators shortly after his arrest that, on the first night they met, he told his father that Suesan had been found dead in the hills after running away. But why were they talking about it anyway?

By an unfortunate twist of fate, Terry's life in Salt Lake City during 1993 was rapidly becoming as unhappy as her mother's was becoming contented. Living in her husband's family's home was stretching the tolerance levels of all concerned, and police were being called to the house with even more regularity than before.

Terry's only escape had been the job at Albertson's. But, if she did catch a glimpse of her mother, then that must have turned into a dreaded place as well.

Then there was Terry's desperation to have children. She was convinced that having a baby might turn her life around. But she also knew that her mother had crushed her stomach so many times that she would have to continue having medical tests before she would know if she could even get pregnant. Also, Terry was worried that having a child might reopen a much more dangerous scenario. She feared that, if she did have children, they might end up being abused in the same awful way that she was. Terry was frightened that her mother might have handed down that propensity for violence to her only surviving daughter. Like mother, like daughter. The very thought haunted her, and it almost resulted in a disaster when a close friend asked Terry if she would look after her two children for a couple of days while her friend went off on a romantic weekend with her husband. Terry agreed because she felt she owed her friend a favour, and she also longed to be in the company of children whom she presumed had actually had a real childhood instead of the brutal regime she had faced day in, day out within the Knorr household.

In fact, Terry was positively excited by the prospect of looking after the youngsters. If anyone had romanticised the very notion of parenthood, it was Terry.

But the first night of looking after those children almost turned into a tragedy. Leaving one of the children alone in the living room while she cooked a meal in the kitchen, Terry did not notice the little boy creep down the stairs to the living quarters of the house in Sandy she shared with her in-laws.

Within minutes she smelled burning. Emerging from the kitchen, she rushed down the spiral staircase and found the little boy in the process of setting fire to her husband's stereo with a box of matches. At first, Terry felt the urge to strike out at the boy.

But then she stopped herself.

She thought she would have been justified in hitting the child, but she also feared what it might lead to. So, instead of harming the child, she immediately made arrangements to get the boy taken elsewhere.

The incident made Terry feel very vulnerable. She had managed to hold herself back from repeating her mother's alleged sins. She knew that, traditionally, the abused child tends to end up abusing his or her own children. She wanted to prove she had broken the cycle.

Terry also had to face another aspect of her abuse at the hands of her mother. She still had not brought that woman to justice. God knows, she had tried hard enough.

Watching television one night, she found herself glued to the show *America's Most Wanted*. Many of the criminals on the lam featured on the programme that night had committed crimes even longer ago than Theresa Knorr. She was particularly fascinated by one case in which the tipster bypassed all the usual police officials and went directly to the actual investigators to get some action taken. Terry realised that charges could still be brought against her mother, but she would have to get to the right people.

This time she would do it. She would actually make the first move to get her mother finally brought to justice. No more half-hearted chats with psychiatrists. No more tearful confessions to friends. This time she would directly call the police department that would have dealt with the deaths of her two sisters.

Terry took a map book off the shelf in that dark and dingy house in Sandy and started to look for the town of Truckee, California ...

FIFTEEN

'As sick as her love was, she was my mother and the only person I knew as loving me.'

TERRY, ONLY SURVIVING DAUGHTER

Police Sergeant Ron Perea, of the Nevada County, California, Sheriff's Office, was used to taking phone calls from all sorts of weirdos, but there was something about the female voice on the other end of the line that had a ring of authenticity about it.

The caller said that her name was Terry Knorr and her two sisters had been killed some years earlier and their bodies dumped in the Nevada County area. Then Terry mentioned that one of her sisters' remains had been left in a box. Sergeant Perea immediately remembered the girl the Texan serial killer had confessed to killing, and his initial impression of the caller altered. Maybe she was just another make-up artist, an attention seeker. After all, they had closed that case years earlier.

Then Terry mentioned the fate of her other sister, and Perea's ears pricked up again because he knew that his colleagues in neighbouring Placer County still had an open investigation on a charred corpse found about eight years previously.

At 10.00 a.m. the following morning, 28 October 1993, Sergeant Perea called up Sergeant John Fitzgerald at the Tahoe City substation of the Placer County Sheriff's Office, told him about the call from Terry and gave him her phone number.

Fitzgerald – forty-six years old, brawny, Brobdingnagian, his moustache freshly trimmed, in his favourite brown tweed sports jacket – was crisply authoritative, a master of cop jargon with a soft, friendly centre.

'I'll get right on it.'

The detective instantly knew precisely which unsolved case Perea's caller was referring to. He had joined the Tahoe substation as a detective just a year after the discovery of the body. Also, he had only just printed up some brand-new flyers with a specially enhanced photograph of Jane Doe #4873/84, prepared from autopsy photographs by the National Center for Missing and Exploited Children in Arlington, Virginia. The poster, headlined do you know her? also featured photos of Suesan's ring and one of her earrings.

Fitzgerald picked up the phone almost immediately and tried to contact Terry Knorr. There was no reply. He tried again later in the day – still no answer.

Raised in Panama – his grandfather helped build the canal – John Fitzgerald had an interesting and varied life history. His

156

family settled in the US from Ireland four generations back. He went to a small private school. Then, just as he was about to go to college, the Vietnam War came along. 'I was a plane captain in the Navy on the USS *Independence* aircraft carrier,' he explained. 'That's the guy who's in charge of a particular plane, inspecting it before and after service.' He spent four years in Vietnam, and placed that experience in an interesting perspective by commenting, 'Basically, I saw no action. I was out at sea the whole time.' After his discharge in 1970, he enrolled in college and became a reserve police officer. He studied criminal justice, graduated from Sierra College, near Auburn, California, and went to work for the Rosewood Police Department, just east of Sacramento. Fitzgerald was anxious to make his mark, but he wanted to do it cleanly, without owing favours and without compromising his ethics. He was a true son of the 1960s.

Fitzgerald moved over to work for the Plumas County Police Department before switching to the Roosevelt Police Department, and then took the job of detective up at the Placer County Sheriff's Department. Married for the second time, with five children between him and his wife, Fitzgerald is a cop with a heart that he openly wears on the sleeve of his always immaculately pressed shirt.

At 4.45 p.m. that day, a female came on the phone who identified herself as Terry Knorr. Close to tears, she repeated her account of life under her tyrannical mother and the eventual tragedy of her sisters' killings.

As Fitzgerald later recalled, 'She started talking and talking. I'd call it non-stop verbal diarrhoea.' Fitzgerald sat on the other end of the line, transfixed by the gruesome account of life in Sacramento. Terry disclosed incidents like being locked in a freezer, having knives thrown at them, being handcuffed to the table and beaten, being hung from the door, suffering regular kickings from her mother, being burned by cigarettes. Then she spoke about the force-feeding, the hot bowl burning the inside of her sister's legs, the molestation by her father, the time her mother stood on her sister's neck.

Terry even gave Fitzgerald the locations where all this occurred: 5539 Bellingham Way, Orangevale, and then the tiny house off 2410 Auburn Boulevard.

'She was very excitable. She was fed up of people not listening to her. She desperately wanted to get the whole thing off her chest,' said Fitzgerald.

Then, weeping periodically, Terry went into graphic detail about the deaths of her two sisters, even describing how the family was spooked when that bird hit the windscreen on the way back from burning Suesan's body.

The conversation went on for an hour and a half. Towards the end of the call, Fitzgerald started to test the authenticity of her claims by asking Terry questions that only someone close to the case of the burned body at Squaw Valley could possibly know.

'Describe to me the ring that your sister was wearing,' asked Fitzgerald.

'It had three rows of diamonds,' came the accurate reply.

'What about other jewellery?'

'She had earrings with bells on them.'

And so it went. Every time Fitzgerald asked a tricky question, Terry came back with the perfect answer. Fitzgerald was fairly certain about Terry. But there was one final question about his Jane Doe that had always baffled him and all the detectives who had handled the case over the years.

'Why did she have those diapers in her possession?' asked the detective.

Terry's reply set her off on yet another graphic description, this time of Suesan's miserable last few weeks of existence.

For John Fitzgerald, this was a major breakthrough on a case he had personally continued to pursue even though it had remained unsolved for more than nine years. He knew that Terry's sister Suesan had to be that Jane Doe Case #4873/84.

In an extraordinary coincidence, he had only just been in touch with the producers of TV's *America's Most Wanted* to ask them to run a segment about that Jane Doe in a last desperate effort to try and identify her.

Suddenly, out of nowhere, a homicide investigation was about to take a dramatic turn.

'This time something will be done,' Fitzgerald assured Terry. 'I want to come and talk to you in person. I'll call you tomorrow.'

At 10.00 a.m. the next morning, John Fitzgerald drove his

grey Ford Explorer along the winding lane that leads past a dozen trailers to the tiny house attached to the apartment block just off Auburn Boulevard, where Terry said she had witnessed death and destruction at the hands of her mother and brothers.

When he got no reply from the house, he tracked down Fern Drake, the manager of the complex, and asked her if she recalled whether a family called the Knorrs had ever lived at the house.

'That name sounds familiar. It must have been them that rented the place. I evicted them eight years back,' explained Fern, who assured Fitzgerald she would try and locate her rental records to confirm the exact dates the family lived at the house.

Next, Fitzgerald headed for the house on Bellingham Way, Orangevale. That also checked out.

By 3.00 p.m. that afternoon, John Fitzgerald was completely and utterly convinced that Terry's claims were accurate. He contacted Inspector Johnnie Smith, his boss at the Placer County Sheriff's headquarters in Auburn, and advised him of all the details.

Smith – a twenty-six-year vet with a droll sense of humour and a sharp eye for detail – felt a chill run up the back of his neck the moment he heard the name Theresa Knorr.

'Hell. I worked a case involving her back in eighty three,' he told an astonished Fitzgerald.

Smith then recounted that interview with Theresa Knorr about her sister's murder and the subsequent surveillance operation on the house just off Auburn. The moment he had made the connection, he told Fitzgerald that they should both get up to Salt Lake City as quickly as possible.

Terry Groves (her married name) was surprised, but also relieved to hear from Fitzgerald that afternoon that he and Smith were flying up the very next day. She was actually starting to believe that her mother might really be brought to justice.

At 7.00 a.m. the next morning, 30 October, John Fitzgerald met Johnnie Smith at the Placer County Sheriff's Department in Auburn and set off to Sacramento Airport in Fitzgerald's Ford Explorer. It was the day before Halloween and Fitzgerald had become embroiled in an alleged double murder that, if true, would turn out to be as gruesome and satanistic as those devil worshippers in Salem, Massachusetts, who sparked the tradition of Halloween three hundred years earlier.

By 1.15 p.m. the two detectives were knocking on the tatty white front door of the house in Sandy, near Salt Lake City, where Terry lived with husband Mike and her in-laws. She greeted them and took them downstairs to the basement annex where she lived, and made them a cup of coffee.

Both detectives were intrigued to finally be meeting Terry. She was more upbeat than they had expected. Somehow, through all that pain and anguish, she still had lively, sparkling blue eyes and a round, healthy face.

For at least fifteen minutes all three made polite small talk, managing to awkwardly avoid mentioning the very subject the two cops had flown from California to discuss. The niceties were harshly broken when one of the cops asked Terry if she had any children.

'Nope. Probably can't have 'em because of the beatings she gave me.'

Smith and Fitzgerald looked stunned for a moment. That was the signal. Fitzgerald placed his Dictaphone on the table in front of them and they began the interview.

Terry took them through her entire childhood. Most of it was pretty grim stuff. It seemed as though beatings were carried out on a daily basis. After Terry had described the killings, Fitzgerald started questioning her about certain evidence taken from the area near Suesan's body. As he showed her photographs of her dead sister's jewellery, she spotted Suesan's ring. It sparked a vision in Terry's mind. She shouted at Fitzgerald and Smith, 'This is my sister's ring. I want that ring.'

'This is a black and white picture of a ring,' said Fitzgerald calmly and carefully, so that it would be clearly stated on the tape recorder.

'I want that ring,' repeated Terry emotionally.

A few moments later, through all the gruesome details of her life, Terry even identified the Budweiser beer can found close to her sister's charred remains.

Terry was fascinated by that flyer Fitzgerald had printed up only a few weeks before her call. She told the investigators that the specially enhanced photograph looked more like her than her sister Suesan.

Three and a half hours after turning on the Dictaphone, the two detectives decided to wind up the interview. They were certain they had both just embarked on the most appalling double homicide investigation either of them had ever encountered.

'I'm going to be working this case and nothing else till we solve it. I promise you,' Fitzgerald told Terry as he and Smith left the house that day. He knew she needed constant reassurance.

The details described by Terry had been so riveting and outrageous that neither detective had kept a close eye on the time, and they had less than an hour to get to Salt Lake City Airport, check in and board the 6.00 p.m. flight back to Sacramento. The journey to the airport in their rented white compact was a hairy ride through thick rush-hour traffic. They got there with only minutes to spare.

At 10.00 a.m. the next day, safely back in his office at the Tahoe City substation, Fitzgerald called Terry in Sandy to run over a few more points that had arisen after he began analysing his lengthy interview with her the previous day. Essentially, he needed background details like the places where both sisters had been born. Once again he assured Terry that this time something would be done.

'We will find your mother, I promise you,' said Fitzgerald.

He then contacted District Attorney Dan Dong to tell him the details of the case. Fitzgerald followed this by starting extensive background checks on Theresa Knorr and her two sons. Terry had given him dates of births, but they had no locations for either Theresa Knorr or Robert, and only a vague area for William. Within hours they located William's workplace and put a surveillance unit on him for a few days to see how he led his life.

Fitzgerald also got in touch with Kelly Keon, the current occupant of that little house just off Auburn Boulevard where so much terror was allegedly inflicted by Theresa Knorr. She immediately agreed to Fitzgerald's request to come and inspect the premises the following day.

At 1.30 p.m. the next day, 1 November, Smith and Fitzgerald met with their boss, Sheriff Don Nunes. Their biggest problem was which force should be responsible for the investigation. Sheila's body had actually been found in Nevada County. But, argued Smith and Fitzgerald, her murder had allegedly been committed in that house, and the family had travelled through Placer County on their way to the dump site. Eventually, after some more discussion, it was agreed that Placer County should run the entire operation.

They decided to immediately set up a task force consisting of Smith, Fitzgerald, and Lieutenant Chal DeCecco.

Case status: Open. Investigation to continue, wrote Fitzgerald in his Placer County Sheriff's Department report at the end of that day.

At 8.00 a.m. the next morning, Fitzgerald, Smith and DeCecco – the Knorr investigation task force – met at the Placer County Sheriff's Department in Auburn to discuss how to handle the case enquiries. It was decided that Fitzgerald and DeCecco would:

- examine the floor of the cupboard where Sheila had been kept prisoner;
- try to obtain photographs of both girls from the schools they attended;
- visit the cinema where Billy Bob had been employed during the time of the alleged murders;
- contact the Department of Justice and the Sacramemo Post Office to try and get a current location for Theresa Knorr.

Numerous other tasks were discussed at that meeting, but the detectives agreed that these four enquiries were top priority.

The rest of that morning was spent running computer checks on Theresa and Robert Knorr in an attempt to hunt them down. Fitzgerald and DeCecco also visited La Entrada School and the Mira Loma School, where they obtained photographs of Suesan Knorr and Sheila Sanders.

At 4.00 p.m. Fitzgerald and DeCecco went to the house off Auburn Boulevard and found, to their disappointment, that the interior of the property had been completely redesigned since the fire lit by Terry more than seven years earlier. However, Fitzgerald did find the cupboard in the hallway where he believed poor Sheila must have been kept prisoner. It had been neatly carpeted over.

Fitzgerald explained to the new tenant, Kelly Keon, that he would like to remove the floor from the closet because it might be possible evidence. She readily agreed, and an arrangement was made for officers to return the next day.

Kelly Keon was very co-operative with the detectives and even told them she would leave the key to the front door by her tap out front so they could let themselves in the next day because she would be out.

That same afternoon, the two investigators contacted Donna Treibel, the manager of the movie theater on Ethan Way where Billy Bob had worked. She could not get access to records to confirm his previous employment, but Fitzgerald was more interested in the shapes and colours of the popcorn-cup boxes delivered to the cinema. He accompanied Donna to the storeroom of the cinema, only to find that the boxes were nothing like the one used to transport Sheila's body. However, Donna then suggested that she might have the kind of box Fitzgerald was looking for at her own house. She promised to get back to him the following day. The investigation was on track again.

The next day, 3 November, Fitzgerald made his first breakthrough in trying to track down Theresa Knorr. A computer check came up with her name under a Utah driver's licence with an address of 2090 Michigan Avenue, Salt Lake City.

Fitzgerald was astounded. Mother and daughter appeared to be living just a few miles from each other. He immediately contacted the Salt Lake City Police Department, spoke with Detective Jill Candland and asked her if a check could be made on that address at Michigan Avenue. She called back a short time later, having been unable to come up with anything that would link Theresa Knorr to that property.

Detective Candland promised to make further checks and assured Fitzgerald she would get back to him within a couple of days.

It was frustrating for the Knorr task force. For every three steps forward, they seemed to take two steps back. But that is the nature of these sorts of inquiries. It's painstaking and it's slow, but you hope to get there in the end.

On the same afternoon, Donna Treibel, manager of the cinema, called Fitzgerald to confirm Billy Bob's employment there. But the box she found at home seemed to be too small to be the kind that the detective was looking for. Once again Fitzgerald felt a twinge of disappointment.

Then, purely as an afterthought, Donna mentioned that a girlfriend of William Knorr's still worked at the cinema. Fitzgerald's enthusiasm jumped right back into gear.

The pieces in the jigsaw were beginning to fit together. The investigation was gaining momentum. Fitzgerald just had to keep it going in the right direction.

On the morning of 4 November 1993, the investigators filed felony complaint number A27527 in the Placer County Municipal Court, alleging two violations of the section 187(a) of the California Penal Code, MURDER and two violations of sections 182(a) (1)/187(a) of the California Penal Code, CONSPIRACY TO COMMIT MURDER for victims Suesan Marline Knorr and Sheila Gay Sanders. The complaint further alleged the special circumstances of MULTIPLE MURDERS and MURDER WAS ESPECIALLY HEINOUS pursuant to California Penal Code sections 190.2 (a) (3) and 190.2(a) (14).

(On November 16 that original complaint was refiled with the special circumstance of MURDER WAS ESPECIALLY HEINOUS deleted and replaced by TORTURE MURDER.)

That afternoon, as planned, Fitzgerald, DeCecco and a maintenance crew including special evidence technicians let themselves into the house just off Auburn Boulevard. As evidence technicians Kelly Yarborough and Tammy Harris snapped furiously away with their cameras, the crew began to remove the floor of the closet very slowly and gently so as not to risk ruining any vital evidence.

Meanwhile, in the basement, DeCecco and Fitzgerald used hand spotlights to methodically check for any further clues. Inside both their minds was the fear that maybe there would be other bodies. Thankfully, that was not the case.

A few minutes later, John Fitzgerald found himself watching the entire cupboard-floor-removal operation in an almost trancelike state. He could not stop thinking about Terry's vivid description of her sister's withered and crushed body crumpled up in that foetal position. Those haunting visions also reminded him that Terry had mentioned how the cupboard had a door handle that could only be locked from the outside. He looked at the cupboard the technicians were so painstakingly removing: it had no such handle.

Fitzgerald then noticed another much smaller cupboard at the other side of the hallway. It could not have been more than two feet by two and a half feet. He looked inside and saw that it had several shelves. Then he examined the door and realised it had a lock that could easily be the same one as Terry had described.

Fitzgerald went back to examine the other, larger cupboard. He was starting to doubt his mind. There was only one way to be absolutely sure. He picked up the phone and called Terry in Salt Lake City.

'It's the smaller one just outside the bathroom on the right side,' was all Terry had to tell Fitzgerald to assure him that his instincts were correct.

The evidence technicians were stunned when Fitzgerald told them to start all over on the smaller cupboard. None of them could believe that any human being existed in such a small space.

SIXTEEN

'Homicide is a function of both person and
circumstance. We are all capable of killing under
some circumstances, and none of us kills
under all circumstances.'

CHARLES PATRICK EWING, AUTHOR

On the west side of Sacramento, at the Target Ware
house Distribution Center in Woodland, two Placer
County investigators were speaking to a very curious
William Knorr about the death of his aunt, Rosemary Norris,
in 1983. The entire interview was conducted purely to sound
out Knorr, to see how he would react to an approach by a
police officer.

'He was fine. Acted completely normally. He did not have
any idea why we were really there,' said one of the
investigators later.

But then why should William Knorr be suspicious? He had
turned over a new leaf, married a pretty girl, settled down in a
comfortable home and avoided all criminal temptations. He

had gone his way and Robert had gone in completely the opposite direction. William had a safe, secure life now ... for the moment.

At 5.00 p.m. that same day, Fitzgerald went and saw William's one-time live-in lover Emily Lewis at the cinema where she still worked. She told Fitzgerald she no longer knew Billy Bob but was able to recall conversations she had with him about his sister's disappearance. She also gave the detective some important information about where Knorr had worked at other jobs.

At precisely the same time, investigators Smith and Fulenwider were knocking on the door of apartment 38, 9127 Newhall Drive, Sacramento – the home of Theresa Knorr's oldest son, Howard Sanders.

Thirty years old and about to embark on his second marriage, Howard Sanders was disarmingly frank in his statement to Smith and Fulenwider. The two policemen started the interview on a traditional softly, softly approach, building gradually up to the most important points.

About fifteen minutes into the interview, Johnnie Smith decided to press Howard harder about the realities of life inside the Knorr household. It was subtle but very effective:

SMITH: I got the feeling that you wanted to tell us something. You said there had been some weird things happening in your family.
SANDERS: Yeah, well ...

SMITH: What is weird that's happened that you wanted to talk about?

SANDERS: Well, you know, there's been a lot of, you know, a lot of problems in our family, you know, we all should be pretty much a loony tune ...

The two detectives hoped that marked the point when they broke through Howard Sanders's reticence. But even they could not have realised just how much he was going to tell them.

When Sanders faltered again about thirty minutes later as he discussed the witchcraft inside the house, Inspector Smith, dour yet determined, would not let him off the hook. The investigator even referred to how he had taken lessons in body language: 'I still think there's something that you want to tell me that you're holding back ...'

It worked because Sanders eventually opened up such a vast torrent of revelations that the two detectives could barely keep up as Sanders mentioned beatings, burnings, whippings and his own disturbing admission about committing incest with Terry.

But there was one more aspect that neither Smith nor Fulenwider had even the remotest clue about. In another interview with Sanders thirteen days later, he admitted sexually abusing his brother Robert as well as Terry.

Even these two hardened detectives were stunned by his confession. Charges of sexual abuse had been there all the time, like a fire deep in the hold of a ship, sending wisps of smoke and acrid smells curling to the deck. But now this throbbing menace was about to explode without warning and roar up hidden passageways to sink the entire vessel. By admitting those awful sexual attacks on his brother and sister, Howard Sanders was trying at last to deal with it and then hopefully put out the flames forever.

The following day, Fitzgerald met at the Sheriff's Department with his colleagues Johnnie Smith, Chal DeCecco and Detective Karl Fulenwider. After discussing their follow-up tasks, they made arrangements to meet with the district attorney in order to obtain a search warrant for William Knorr's home. They also needed to arrange for the issuing of arrest warrants for all three suspects: Theresa Jimmie Knorr, William Robert Knorr and Robert Wallace Knorr.

Later that morning, John Fitzgerald gave a verbal affidavit to Judge Garbolino at the courthouse in Auburn and officially obtained the search warrant plus the arrest warrants. It was decided that an arrest should be made of William Knorr as quickly as possible, in case he was tipped off about the murder inquiries. Investigators had got to the point where they did not know where the other brother and the mother were, so they needed to arrest William promptly.

At 2.00 p.m. that afternoon, all four detectives travelled to the Target Warehouse Distribution Center in Woodland to arrest William Knorr. Smith drove in his small blue four-door Mercury with Fulenwider, while Fitzgerald and DeCecco travelled in the Explorer. On arrival at the plant, all four detectives initially feared their suspect was not at work because there was no sign of his car in the company parking lot. But, when Smith and his partner went into the personnel office, they were told that Knorr was at work. He had been given a ride in by a friend. The manager was then asked to page Knorr without informing him what it was about. The other two investigators sealed off the rear exit to the building in case Knorr tried to flee.

Five minutes later a bemused-looking William Knorr arrived in the front office, where Johnnie Smith approached him.

'We have a warrant for your arrest,' Smith told Knorr.

It took a few moments to sink in. Then William Knorr surprised the officers by asking them if he could call the guy he car-pooled with to tell him not to bother coming by to pick him up on the way home that evening. That was his main concern, rather than the fact he was under arrest for murder.

Three minutes after that, a grim-faced William Knorr was led from the building, where he was turned over by Smith to Fitzgerald and DeCecco, who read Knorr 821/822 of the Penal Code regarding magistrate's advisement. Knorr immediately agreed to accompany the officers to the Placer County Sheriff's Department. They snapped a pair of handcuffs on his wrists.

The two detectives began to interview Know virtually the moment the three got in Fitzgerald's gun-metal-grey Explorer, and read him his Miranda rights. He was astonished to discover that the interview about his aunt's death the previous day had just been an excuse to get close to him.

During the thirty-minute ride from Woodland to Auburn, Knorr told the detectives that both his sisters had disappeared and he had no idea where his mother or brother were now living. He talked openly about how his mother had abused all the children, and even confirmed that she did own the Ford LTD Terry had mentioned in her statement. But Knorr was in complete denial as far as the deaths of his two sisters were concerned. He would not concede anything about them.

Then, just as Fitzgerald drove the Explorer through Auburn towards the Sheriff's Department on the other side of town, William Knorr mentioned that he had been threatened with death by his mother if he ever tried to leave the family unit.

The two investigators sat in silence, hoping he would elaborate. But William Knorr did not say anything more. Moments later they parked outside the Sheriff's Department.

On arrival inside the building, DeCecco escorted William Knorr to the investigation interview room. Knorr was being fairly co-operative, but still not candid about the actual allegations against him. A tape recorder and a video camera were permanently set up in the room to monitor all interviews.

William Knorr flatly denied any involvement in the disappearance of Sheila or Suesan. Then Fitzgerald and DeCecco advised him that they had already interviewed his sister Terry and half-brother Howard.

'We kinda put our cards on the table,' said John Fitzgerald, ever the master of the understatement. 'We wanted him to know that we knew what had happened.'

William Knorr looked worried. He immediately recalled for the two investigators a number of incidents inside the Knorr household, even claiming Suesan was out of control and turning tricks as a prostitute and that was why Theresa Knorr started beating her. He talked about how Suesan was trapped under the table on that kitchen floor.

William Knorr insisted to the detectives that, when they took Suesan off into the mountains, his mother had simply informed them that they were 'going on a car ride'. He also said – contrary to what Terry claimed – that Terry was in the car with them. He confirmed that the first trip had been aborted, and told them about loading Suesan into his mother's Ford LTD the next day and once again setting off east on Interstate 80.

John Fitzgerald later confronted Terry about her brother's claims that she had been in the car when both her sisters were dumped. She denied it categorically.

William Knorr even admitted to the two officers that he doused his sister in petrol and then lit the fatal match. For the second time, he insisted his mother had threatened him with death if he should decide to tell anyone about that night's activities.

'What about Sheila?' the investigators asked their suspect.

William claimed he was once again ordered to help dispose of her by his evil mother. William said Sheila was not alive when they removed her body from the cupboard.

Then he revealed that, just before the family dumped Sheila, they stopped by the side of the road to look for potential locations to leave the box containing her body and were spotted by a passing police cruiser. As the two brothers scanned the bleak and darkened terrain a few yards from the Ford LTD, two patrolman approached Theresa Knorr, who was still sitting behind the wheel. They asked her what she was doing out in a deserted area late at night.

'The two boys are just over there urinating,' came Theresa Knorr's very calm reply.

The two policemen accepted her response and did not even stop to inspect the contents of the boot of that car. If they had opened it up, they would have found the box containing Sheila's withered corpse and prevented her alleged killers from keeping their liberty for eight more years.

As the interview at the sheriff's headquarters drew to a close, William Knorr insisted to the investigators that he had cut himself off from the family and did not want to remember any more facts about the deaths of his two sisters. But he did admit that he had not intended to ever tell authorities about the two deaths.

Meanwhile, Smith and Fulenwider travelled to William Knorr's home at 4016 Tressler Avenue, North Highlands, where they told his wife, DeLois Ann Knorr, that her husband had just been arrested for murder. She was stunned by the news, but agreed to help detectives with some background information.

DeLois – a pretty, slimly built blonde with a preference for neat, tight-fitting power suits and two-inch heels – told the investigators she had never met William's mother and that her husband had told her that she had been very abusive towards the children.

She also revealed to detectives that William Knorr had told her that one of his sisters had been climbing on a shelf after being ordered to do so by his mother and that his sister fell and broke her neck.

By 3:35 p.m. Fulenwider and Smith were executing their search warrant at William Knorr's home after reassuring a very shocked DeLois that it had to be done.

An hour later the two investigators encountered Robert Knorr Sr., who had been alerted to the situation by DeLois. His first response to the detectives was not horror at the news of the arrests, but a mild concern that two of the Veterans' Administration payment cheques sent to Theresa Knorr to help Terry once she turned eighteen had been returned.

Knorr Sr. informed detectives that, apart from William, he had not seen his kids in seventeen years. Then the father of Suesan Knorr told investigators that Theresa Knorr never liked Sheila. He insisted that his ex-wife had hit and beaten Sheila on a regular basis, and he recalled one particular incident when Sheila was about three years old and Theresa Knorr beat the little girl's head so hard against a wall he had had to intervene.

Neither of the investigators responded openly to Knorr's remarks, but privately they were starting to wonder why no one had ever brought Theresa Knorr to justice years before she allegedly began killing her daughters.

Back at the Placer County Sheriff's Department, methodical computer checks had finally uncovered a possible location for Robert Knorr – the Nevada State Jail, at Ely. No one was that surprised to find Robert was already incarcerated for the murder of a bartender, completely unconnected with the abuse and killings alleged to have taken place inside the Knorr household. Or was it?

The Knorr task force decided not to rush across the state line to interview Robert. He had nowhere to run. Their main priority was to locate Theresa Knorr before she completely disappeared under a haze of false names and disguises.

At 2:30 p.m. the following day, 5 November, Fitzgerald and DeCecco went to see William Knorr, this time in his cell at the Placer County Jail attached to the main courtrooms in Auburn. Again William was read his Miranda rights before DeCecco switched on a Dictaphone minicassette recorder.

The two detectives wanted to go over some of the other details surrounding Knorr's sisters' deaths, like the type of duct tape used to wrap around Suesan's body and across her mouth. Knorr insisted that he could not remember any shooting incident involving Suesan or any other wounds inflicted by his mother or Suesan.

He did talk about the dreadful, last beating inflicted on Sheila by her mother, and he referred to the locations where the bodies were dumped after being shown a number of crime-scene photos by Fitzgerald.

That same day, the Placer County Sheriff's Department issued a two-page press release to inform the world of the extraordinary double murder inquiry. Written in heavy, bold-type capital letters, it began:

SHERIFF DONALD J. NUNES RELEASES THE
FOLLOWING INFORMATION:
SHERIFF NUNES ANNOUNCED TODAY THAT A 1984
HOMICIDE, ONE OF THE MOST ALARMING AND
BIZARRE IN THE HISTORY OF PLACER COUNTY, HAS
BEEN RESOLVED ...

The release went on to notify the media of all the case's basic
details and then signed off with a piece of guessology that
was pretty close to the mark:

THERESA KNORR MAY BE EMPLOYED, OR SEEKING
EMPLOYMENT, AT A CONVALESCENT HOSPITAL.

That same day, Fitzgerald – still very concerned that he had
no concrete clues as to where Theresa Knorr was living –
contacted police in Washoe County, Nevada, to see if they
could locate her in the Reno area. He had been told by
prison officials in Ely that Robert Knorr had tried to contact
his mother at an address in Reno. Detective Dick
Williamson, of the Washoe County Sheriff's Department,
assured Fitzgerald he would do everything possible to help
try and track down Theresa Knorr, and promised to get
back to him as quickly as possible.

Fitzgerald also contacted Terry once again to discuss the
progress he was making. He asked her to make a list of all the
incidents of abuse suffered by her and her sisters at the
hands of their mother and two brothers, William and Robert.

Then Fitzgerald told Terry he would be in touch with her 'in a few weeks'. The investigator's words summed up Terry's worst fears. When he said 'a few weeks', she began to wonder if the police were really that interested. The lack of urgency in Fitzgerald's response worried her. She had come this far. She wanted action to be taken immediately. But they still had not even located her mother. She was very, very worried.

SEVENTEEN

'You know all she did was screw her own life.
For Christ's sake, do you think, I mean, if I had,
I mean I'm going right now through surgeries to try
to have children because of the abuse. My insides
were mangled from this woman. Yet, my mother
also did some wonderful things.'

TERRY KNORR

'I'll get you. I know where you are.'
The male voice on the other end of the telephone was
calm, dry and very menacing. Terry was extremely nervous.
She slammed the handset down without uttering a word. It
had only been a few hours since Sergeant Fitzgerald had
informed her he would be in touch with her in a few weeks.

In a few weeks I could be dead, thought Terry.

A couple of minutes later – at just about 9.00 p.m. on 5
November 1993 – the telephone rang again. This time Terry
hesitated to pick it up. But it kept on ringing relentlessly.
She succumbed.

'I'll get you. I know where you are.'

She slammed it down again. This time Terry was petrified.

She picked up the phone and called the local police department at Sandy and got through to desk duty officer Jeff Duval.

Within a few hours he had placed a flag on the house, just in case any strangers were lurking nearby.

The following morning, thirty-four-year-old Sandy Police Department detective David Lundberg was enjoying a lazy Saturday at home when his sergeant, Eddie Kantor, called to ask him if he would be prepared to talk to a lady about some threatening phone calls that she claimed were linked to the murder of her two sisters.

'We need to look into this to see if there is anything in it,' Kantor told Lundberg.

The young detective was intrigued. He called Terry at the number she had left with Officer Duval the previous evening. Lundberg listened patiently for more than an hour as she poured out her life story once again.

After getting off the phone with Terry, Lundberg immediately contacted John Fitzgerald in Placer County, who confirmed the existence of the task force. Both cops assumed that Terry's plea to her local police was an attempt to guarantee that this time something really was going to be done.

Lundberg went into the Sandy Police Department that Saturday morning and did some computer checks on Terry's home address. He soon discovered that police had been called to the house on at least a dozen occasions and, only two weeks earlier, Terry had even spent a night in jail after an altercation with a patrolman who tried to break up a domestic disturbance at the house.

David Lundberg's devotion was typical of a man with a very clear sense of right and wrong. The youngest of nine kids brought up in Salt Lake City, the dapper detective wanted to be a cop 'because I got into a lot of trouble as a kid and decided it might be kinda fun to join the other side'. His problems included involvement in drugs, hanging out and drinking beer. Then he did two years at college studying law enforcement and joined the Sandy Police Department. Married life beckoned once ... for just three months. 'Thank God it was a quick one.' By this time he was sharing his neat house on the edge of Sandy with a couple of cats and a dog.

Lundberg's biggest case was the Alta View Hospital siege in Sandy in 1990. 'They made a TV movie out of that one,' he says proudly. Then a young patrolman, Lundberg arrived on the scene not realising that a siege was in progress, and immediately found himself confronting an armed man who was holding two nurses hostage. The gunman, furious at Lundberg for daring to challenge him, then killed one of the nurses to prove he meant business. 'It was very traumatic.' After eight hours, the siege ended and gunman Richard Worthington was arrested. 'He hung himself in jail recently,' said Lundberg, with just a touch of satisfaction in his voice.

When Lundberg arrived at Terry's place in his tan-coloured Corsica the following Monday morning, he immediately recognised the property as the same place he had visited as a patrolman during yet another of Terry's regular domestic disturbances a year or so earlier.

Terry was relieved to have another policeman take an

interest in her case. The combination of the threatening phone calls and John Fitzgerald's comment about getting back to her in a few weeks had made her feel as if no one really cared.

The young, ambitious detective was even more intrigued when Terry told him she had reported the killings to a sheriff over at Woods Cross three years earlier and that nothing was done. Terry also revealed that she had told one of his colleagues at the Sandy Police Department, who had called at the house following yet another domestic disturbance at least a year earlier.

Lundberg bonded very well with the frightened twenty-three-year-old. He was especially interested in her claims because he had worked on a number of child-abuse cases over the years.

'The more detail she went into, the more convinced I became,' said Lundberg. 'I was fascinated.'

In the background, Terry's in-laws drifted in and out of the room, hardly uttering a word. Lundberg says he felt they were very suspicious of his motives in coming to the house. The detective's only aim was in fact to ensure that this time Terry's claims were properly acted upon. He was also determined to expose the officers from Woods Cross and Sandy who had apparently ignored Terry's plight.

Terry was very impressed by David Lundberg. By the end of their meeting, she felt that the young detective really did care about what she was saying.

Lundberg even gave Terry his home phone number and insisted that she feel free to call him any-time.

'I had a gut feeling about Terry. If I was dealing with a dangerous suspect, then it would be different, but this was a case where she really needed someone to talk to.' As Lundberg left Terry's house, he promised her he would get something done. As they stood on the doorstep, he stopped momentarily and hugged Terry reassuringly. 'If you need anything, call me.'

The moment Lundberg got back to his neat, pristine desk at the ultra-modern, open-plan detectives' bureau at the Sandy Police Department's brand-new headquarters on Centennial Parkway, alongside Interstate 15, he put a request in to find out who interviewed Terry all those years earlier.

The department CAD computer system was supposed to log all police-involved incidents. It records addresses, times, dates and people's names, to provide data to be cross-referenced with police departments across the nation.

Lundberg punched in a request for everything on Terry's home address at Pepperwood Drive. Within minutes he was pouring over the many details of the domestic disputes at the house, but there was no mention of an interview into the deaths of her sisters. Lundberg wondered if Terry had perhaps mentioned it to an officer who wrote it off during one of those many visits by saying she was intoxicated and talking nonsense.

A few days later, after conducting his own unofficial internal enquiries, Lundberg tracked down the Sandy policeman concerned and confronted him.

'He looked me in the face and said he did not recall her

187

saying anything about her sisters,' says Lundberg bitterly. He believes that cop was 'covering his ass like a true professional'.

The next day, Lundberg returned to Terry's home to try and get some more details about her allegations. She was more relaxed because the threatening phone calls had stopped. Terry even admitted her own innermost fears about becoming a child abuser herself. It really worried Terry that she might end up like her mum, and she told him how she had got that friend to take the child away who almost burned down the house when she was babysitting.

Lundberg gave Terry a poster that said love doesn't have to hurt, which featured a photo of a hand holding a rose with just a prick of blood on the forefinger. Below it read: *Domestic Violence Can Stop 1-800-897-LINK*. He knew that, if a similar sort of service had existed a few years earlier, the Knorr tragedy might have been prevented.

Having observed the poverty inside that house on Pepperwood, Lundberg also insisted Terry and her in-laws have his Thanksgiving turkey voucher, awarded to all serving police officers at Sandy as a gesture of thanks from City Hall.

Lundberg believes that Terry was feeling isolated because John Fitzgerald and the Placer County task force were a long distance away. Terry frequently would call him in the middle of the night with a nugget of information she had forgotten to tell him before.

'She was always very apologetic, saying, "I hope I did not disturb you or wake you up."'

Lundberg spent hours one morning making calls to all the hospitals in the Salt Lake City area to find Terry a friendly, sympathetic psychiatrist willing to treat her for no charge. He recognised that she was someone in dire need of professional counselling.

The Nevada State Prison, at Ely, is the sort of place where inmates sometimes bolt across the day-room floor and, at full stride, smash their fists into the side of a prison guard's head, knocking him to the floor.

But the obvious problems of life inside a tough jail had shrunk into insignificance for twenty-four-year-old Robert Wallace Knorr. As he paced up and down the nine-by-nine cell he shared with another inmate, he could not stop thinking about what was happening back in Auburn.

The police had already been in touch with him and asked for his full co-operation. He turned them down flat, and one investigator predicted that authorities were going to have to get a court order to force him to appear in any eventual trial. They already knew that the whole question of whether or not he should be treated as an adult or a child was going to be a crucial part of any court hearing, as he was fifteen and sixteen at the times of his sisters' killings.

A few days after Terry received those threatening phone calls, her mother, Theresa Knorr, noticed the first newspaper and television reports concerning Terry's allegations against her. Sheriff Don Nunes's press release on the investigation into

Sheila's and Suesan's deaths had alerted the world to her alleged crimes.

But it was the local news report on Utah's KUTV Channel 2 that must have shaken even Theresa Knorr to the very core. There, on the television screen, was her only surviving daughter, Terry, telling the world about the awful abuse and murder allegedly inflicted on her family.

Terry, close to tears throughout the interview, told interviewer Peter Rosen, 'What kind of mother would do that? What kind of person am I going to be for the rest of my life because of this?

'All my life I've tried to put out of my mind what happened. I couldn't believe that it actually happened. I just want my sisters to know I had nothing to do with this and I loved them. I don't have them now and I want them back.

'I told all these people, but none of them wanted to believe I was actually telling the truth. They all thought I had loony tunes and that I had problems, well, what the heck do they expect!

'I have asked myself a hundred times why didn't I just tell them to run. I didn't know what to do. All my life I have tried to block it out of my mind.'

The KUTV Channel 2 news show also reported that police were still trying to find Theresa Jimmie Knorr. Fitzgerald had even provided the media with a copy of that almost glamorous photograph of her that she used on her Utah driver's licence. Sheriff Nunes admitted, 'We don't know where she is. She's in the wind somewhere.'

On the morning of November 5, Theresa Knorr got a loan in the form of a check from Bud Sullivan for $4600 to be paid back to him against her salary. He had turned down her initial request a week earlier. But then she came back to him and said she really needed the money. Bud–a relaxed good old boy in his early sixties–asked her why. She told him she had another heavy tax bill to pay, and since she had reliably repaid an earlier loan out of her wages, he reluctantly agreed.

Later that same day, 5 November, Theresa Knorr disappeared from her duties as nurse to Alice Sullivan for the entire afternoon, leaving the old lady stranded at a bridge session some distance from her home. Eventually a barman at the bridge club gave her a ride home and a neighbour took pity on Alice – who suffers from Parkinson's disease – when they found her shivering on her cold porch waiting for Theresa to appear with the front-door key.

On Interstate 15, Theresa Knorr had actually been stopped by Utah State Troopers after being spotted weaving in and out of traffic on the busy motorway.

The troopers studied the Utah driver's licence: Theresa Jimmie Cross, 1296 North 400 East, Bountiful, Utah 84010. Weight: 170. Eyes: Blue. Birth Date: 03/14/ 1946. Height: 5ft. 05in ...

Minutes later she was arrested on suspicion of drunk driving.

At about 6.00 p.m. that evening Theresa finally turned up back at the house in a taxi, claiming her car had broken down on the motorway.

Incredibly, the woman who was by now the most wanted mother in the entire country was released by Utah law enforcement officials because her maiden name was not on the list of aliases put in the national police-wanted computer.

Pat Thatcher and her brother Bud Sullivan had been very concerned by Theresa's absence, but they believed her excuse about the car breaking down and let things ride because she had been such a loyal nurse and friend to the entire family since starting work there the previous year.

When a group of close family members in from Connecticut turned up at Alice's house for a reunion party the next day, nothing more was mentioned about Theresa's car problems.

At the gathering, Theresa seemed relaxed, sipping sedately from a glass of red wine and laughing and joking with the other guests.

Alice's nephew Thom McMahon was most impressed by his aunt's helper. 'When I met her the first time, it was like I'd known her my whole life. She was a very concerned person … very friendly, very warm.'

But, when one of the relatives tried to snap a photo of Theresa Knorr, she slipped conveniently into the background. However, the Thatchers did later manage to get a handful of shots that included Theresa, and she looks the very epitome of a healthy, stable, middle-aged lady.

At the party that Saturday, Theresa made a point of leaving any room each time Pat Thatcher's attractive daughter Shannon walked in. Shannon – who was in her thirties and married, with three beautiful children – seemed to pose a threat to Theresa Cross.

'Shannon felt that Theresa did not like her from the moment they met. Whenever she visited Alice, Theresa would open the door to her and the kids and then go straight to her bedroom and never reappear until after they had gone. It was almost as if she did not want to share the spotlight with someone prettier and younger than her,' recalled Pat.

Old habits die hard …

EIGHTEEN

'What kind of mother could do that? What kind
of person am I going to be throughout my life?
That's what I want to know? How am I going to
deal with it? What's going to happen to me?'

TERRY KNORR

On 6 November 1993, Detective Dick Williamson of the
Washoe County Sheriff's Department proved to John
Fitzgerald that just once in a while cops actually help other
cops without needing an ulterior motive. As he promised he
would, Williamson had tracked down an address in Reno
that he believed to be Theresa Jimmie Knorr's current home.

Fitzgerald and his task force partner Chal DeCecco
immediately made a two-hour dash along Interstate 80 to
the address. It was a bum lead. No one there knew or had
even heard of Theresa Knorr. She may have lived there a few
years back, but she had long since gone.

The main problem facing detectives was that Theresa had
used a long list of aliases over the years, including all of her

married names and a handful of nicknames. From the 1970s they found that she had beaten a bad cheque rap, and then there were the visits by the Child Protective Services for the alleged child-abuse charges she managed to talk her way out of with the same, sweet, guileless charm she displayed on the witness stand in her 1964 murder trial.

In Sacramento, the whole city was suddenly abuzz with news of Theresa Jimmie Knorr's alleged crimes. The *Bee* splashed a headline across its front page that proclaimed: mother sought in grisly slayings, two daughters burned, starved.

Then, on 9 November, Robert Knorr Sr., the father of four of Theresa Knorr's children, decided to go public by agreeing to an interview in the *Bee*. He made it absolutely clear whose side he was on.

'We believe William and we love him and we're behind him a hundred per cent,' said Knorr Sr. in reference to the charges faced by his twenty-six-year-old son.

He spoke to newsmen outside the Placer County Jail on 8 November after attending a preliminary court hearing for William. Alongside him were his daughter-in-law DeLois and a handful of relatives.

Knorr Sr. blamed his ex-wife for all the problems now faced by his sons, and even assured journalists, 'When I left there, I never thought she was really that crazy. But I guess she was. It's a sad story for my children to be treated like this.'

Significantly, Robert Knorr Sr. ignored the claims of abuse made against him by Terry. He even claimed that Terry –

who has made accusations of molestation against him in her statements to Placer County detectives – was not necessarily his daughter.

'I just went ahead and gave her my name, but there is some doubt in my mind.'

Back outside the court, DeLois, who had only ever known the new law-abiding, clean-living version of William, was close to tears as she said, 'We love each other and I'm going to get him home, whatever it takes.'

A few minutes earlier, in the neat, ultra-modern courtroom, Superior Court Judge J. Richard Couzens announced that William Knorr might not even have been properly charged in an adult court. He ordered that the charges had to be first addressed in Juvenile Court, where a determination would be made as to whether he should be tried as an adult.

William Knorr stood, head bowed, barely able to acknowledge the presence of anyone in that courtroom. His only comment to the judge was that his family were attempting to hire a private attorney, former Justice Court Judge Robert A. Young, to handle his defence. Further proceedings were scheduled for 23 November.

On the same day that William was making his first court appearance, Investigator John Fitzgerald got a call from Salt Lake City cops telling him of an address and post office box details for Theresa Cross traced through a driver's licence application she had made in Utah three years earlier. They had even managed to locate the make and registration number of a car she had purchased – all thanks to that drunk-driving arrest five days earlier. This time Fitzgerald and Smith were convinced they were close, and they knew they could not leave it to the Salt Lake City Police to check out the address.

'It's always better to do these sort of jobs yourself,' explained Fitzgerald.

On 9 November they flew on the early-evening flight from Sacramento to Salt Lake City.

At 7.30 a.m. the next morning, after a good night's sleep in their motel rooms, Fitzgerald and Smith headed out to the address on South 600 East where they believed Theresa Knorr was living. They had no idea of the circumstances under which she was existing.

When they got to the house, all appeared quiet. The two cars parked outside did not check out as having any connection to Theresa Knorr and, since her car was not around the two investigators decided to return at a later time. They did not want to alert anyone in the neighbourhood to their presence, and drove off to the Salt Lake City main post office to see if Theresa Knorr was picking up her mail from the PO box she had set up sometime previously.

At the post office, nobody knew what she looked like, and the two detectives considered whether they should just wait and see if she turned up to collect her mail. But that seemed a ludicrous long shot.

'We might have waited a week till she showed up. We did not have that sort of time on our hands,' says Fitzgerald.

The two detectives left their cards and a phone number at the SLCPD just in case Theresa Knorr appeared, and then set off to run down some more leads. A forty-five-mile trip south to the city of Provo proved fruitless, and all their other enquiries were equally unhelpful.

At 4.45 p.m., as darkness fell, Smith and Fitzgerald decided to make another run past the house on South 600 East. As they turned right on to Kensington, which ran alongside the corner property, Fitzgerald spotted Theresa Knorr's red Plymouth, with licence plate 083DBW, parked on the driveway up to the garage.

'Bingo. She's here. She's gotta be,' he told his colleague.

The two detectives then headed off for the nearest public phone to call the Salt Lake City Police Department to request an officer to accompany them on the arrest. They were about to detain someone for a crime committed in another state, and there were certain procedures they needed to go through.

Just then a clearly marked SLCPD cruiser drove past them. Fitzgerald swung his small rental car around and within minutes they had managed to wave down Officer J. D. Whitaker, who actually was not even on duty at the time. Under a new SLCPD scheme, he had been allowed to take the patrol car home on the understanding that, if any crime occurred while he was in the vehicle, he would automatically go back on duty. SLCPD reckon that the mere presence of police cruisers on the streets can prevent crime. It was an admirable scheme.

Whitaker was at first very cautious. He ran a local check on Theresa Knorr and confirmed that everything Smith and Fitzgerald were telling him was true. The two investigators – while appreciating the young patrolman's reservations – were anxiously watching the time ticking away, fearful that Knorr might leave the house if they did not get back there very rapidly. After some more discussion, Whitaker agreed to accompany .the two detectives to the house on South 600 East Street.

Just before 5.15 p.m. the three police officers parked their cars more than a block and a half away from the Sullivan house just to be on the safe side. They did not want to blow it at this late hour.

Fitzgerald and Whitaker approached the front door of the house while Smith checked out the back. The drapes in the front window were open, and Fitzgerald noticed eighty-six-year-old Alice Sullivan sitting in the front living room, but he could not see any sign of Theresa Knorr. Both investigators were confused by the presence of Alice since they did not even realise that Theresa Knorr was working as a care giver to an elderly lady. Fitzgerald knocked gently, careful not to make it sound like an urgent matter because that might cause the suspect to try and flee. For more than a minute he waited, but there was no reply. He tried again.

Within seconds Theresa Knorr finally answered the door. Fitzgerald hesitated for a moment, before recognising her from her Utah driver's licence photograph. 'She looks a lot better than in her California one, 'cause she's fixed herself,' he recalled thinking. She had lost weight – about sixty pounds – but she was still short and heavy, she still had short brown hair, and her eyes were still alternately as cold as ice and as warm as the sad, sweet smile she used when she wanted something. Then, out of typical old-fashioned courtesy, Fitzgerald asked her, 'Are you Theresa Cross?' She did not reply:

'I am a police officer from the state of California and I need to talk with you.'

'Not in front of the lady. Come this way.'

Theresa Knorr beckoned the two policemen into the house. She was sensitive about the old lady hearing what was happening. Just then, Inspector Smith also appeared and joined them.

Fitzgerald, Smith and Whitaker followed Knorr to the bedroom at the rear of the house. At this stage none of the policemen had even suggested why they needed to talk to Theresa Knorr. She did tell them she preferred the name Cross to Knorr. 'I don't like that name.'

Once they got to the back bedroom, Fitzgerald came clean. 'I have a warrant for your arrest on two counts of murder, and we are placing you under arrest.'

Theresa looked stunned but said nothing. Then she explained to the officers that she needed to contact the son of Alice Sullivan – the old lady she was looking after – so that arrangements could be made to take care of her.

Fitzgerald allowed her to make the call to Bud Sullivan.

'Bud, it's Theresa here, can you come down to your mother's house,' Theresa told him.

Bud knew immediately something was wrong. 'What's the matter?'

'The police are here. They want to arrest me on a warrant.'

'What for?'

'I don't know.'

Theresa Knorr had too much pride to admit to Bud why she was being arrested.

Then the three police officers and the woman accused of committing two of the most horrendous killings in Californian history sat down in the kitchen of the house and made polite conversation while they waited twenty minutes for Bud Sullivan to come over and look after his mum.

Fitzgerald believes that Knorr had seen some of the media coverage about the case on the local TV news and was preparing to disappear and re-emerge in some other city on the other side of the country. She was getting ready to flee, but thought she still had a little time. She was going to get a U-Haul, hook it up to her car, go to the storage shed where she kept her other belongings and then get to the next big city, probably Denver.

Bud Sullivan was still wondering what the problem was as he headed across town with his girlfriend Marji. 'I thought she probably had a bunch of parking tickets. I said to Marji, "We better post her some bail money so we can get her out to carry on looking after mom,"' he later recalled.

When Bud did finally get to the house, John Fitzgerald took him into a back room and said, 'I don't want you to talk to her about this, but she is being arrested on suspicion of murder.'

For a moment Bud was stunned. Then he remembered seeing that report about Terry Knorr and her dead sisters on the television a few days earlier.

Bud walked back into the kitchen where Theresa was calmly leaning against a sideboard.

'I don't know why they are arresting me,' she said. Then silence, followed by an afterthought: 'Will you sell my car for me?'

As is sometimes the case with honourable people, the hunter – in this case Fitzgerald – still had time to sound a little sympathetic towards his prey, Theresa Knorr.

'She was trying to do the best with her life and look more attractive. Wearing nice clothes and all. She wanted to run a clean life and enjoy it without getting involved in any trouble. She did not want to attract any attention to herself,' said Fitzgerald.

It sounded a lot like Billy Bob. He had also tried to start fresh ... until John Fitzgerald came along. Fitzgerald and Smith decided it wasn't necessary to cuff Theresa Knorr inside the Sullivan house. Fitzgerald led her outside by the arm and handcuffed her once they were in the front yard.

He put her in the investigators' four-door rental, and SLCPD Patrolman Whitaker followed closely behind. At 6.20 p.m. Fitzgerald and Smith arrived at the Salt Lake City Police Department with their prisoner. They immediately took her to the interview room on the fifteenth floor, where she was read her Miranda rights by Smith. Theresa Knorr refused to waive those rights and sat in stoney silence. The two investigators knew then that Theresa Knorr was not going to be opening her heart up to them for the time being.

'I want a lawyer' was about all she would say. Within a few minutes Fitzgerald and Smith gave up and decided it was time to leave the room. Fitzgerald went to the door; it was locked. Suddenly it dawned on him that neither he nor Smith had the key, because they were just visiting officers, not actually stationed at the SLCPD.

Theresa Knorr sat stoney-faced at the interview table, unaware of the situation until Fitzgerald started pounding on the door to try and get someone's attention. Two Salt Lake City officers walked past, looked through the glass window and promptly barked at the two California cops: 'Get away from there. You'll be let out when the officer gets back.'

They thought that Smith and Fitzgerald were prisoners.

'In the middle of all this drama and talk about the appalling crimes this woman was alleged to have committed, we had ended up being prisoners in a police station,' recalled Fitzgerald. 'It was ridiculous.'

As Fitzgerald continued pounding on the door, a sly grin came to the face of Theresa Knorr. It was the only time John Fitzgerald ever noticed her smile.

Eventually they got out of the interview room and escorted their prisoner to the Salt Lake County Jail – the same prison where her daughter Terry had been an inmate after her domestic flare-ups at her in-laws' house.

During the four-block drive, Fitzgerald gave Theresa Knorr his business card and said, 'If you change your mind, just call me.' He wanted to be absolutely certain he had done everything possible to elicit a confession. Theresa Knorr took the card and said nothing. In fact, the only thing she talked about on the way to jail that evening was her three sons, Howard, William; and Robert.

But not once, noted John Fitzgerald a few months later, not once did she mention her daughters.

As they arrived at the jail, Theresa Knorr simply said, 'I feel like a sacrificial lamb being led to the slaughter.'

The following day was the Veterans Day holiday, so the two Placer County investigators decided they would spend the day following up more leads, trying to contact people who might actually be at home rather than work.

Over at his mother's house on South 600 East, Bud Sullivan was getting a taste of that much mentioned Andy Warhol phenomenon – fifteen minutes of fame. Masses of TV crews, photographers and reporters had gathered outside the front door for a chat about Theresa Knorr.

Channel 2 proudly reported, 'A murderer has been caught right here in Salt Lake City. The suspect: a forty-seven-year-old woman. The victims: her own two children. The case had been a mystery for almost a decade until a surviving daughter gave cops what they were looking for ...'

Later that day, the hot news was updated to include some footage of the Sullivan house: 'Forty-seven-year-old Theresa Knorr is in Salt Lake County Jail. She was arrested in this Salt Lake home yesterday. Knorr is suspected of killing her two daughters nine years ago in California. According to police, her seventeen-year-old daughter's charred body was found in 1984. A year later in Truckee her other daughter was ...'

In one report, Bud Sullivan – looking distinctly uncomfortable under the 'glare of the camera lights – said: 'It was a complete shock. None of us had any idea about her past.'

Bud Sullivan was still having great difficulty believing any of the things he had heard about Theresa Knorr. One neighbour, Cynthia Russell, talked happily to the TV crews about how her kids used to go over to the house and do odd jobs. 'She was a very nice neighbour. My reaction is that they must have the wrong person or something.'

Inspector Johnnie Smith – head of the Placer County task force formed to bring the Knorrs to justice – privately admitted in an interview in February 1994 that he was just as surprised by Theresa Knorr as those neighbours.

'I was expecting an entirely different type of person after hearing all those evil things about her. She was more refined, she cared for the elderly, she was respected in the community, people were full of praise for her. No one had a bad word to say about her.

'It was as if she had ended one life to start another. In fact, I think that is what she did. She terminated that evil life and headed for Reno, then Salt Lake.'

Reporters even traced Howard Sanders, who, after learning of his mother's arrest, said, 'I'm really glad they caught her; I'm relieved. Maybe they can go forward now and find out exactly what went on. Nobody else can be hurt.'

At 9.15 a.m. that same morning, Bud Sullivan got a call from Fitzgerald and Smith, who wanted to know how he came to hire Theresa Cross, as she was known to him.

Sullivan admitted, rather embarrassed, that he had loaned Theresa Cross $4600 after she told him she needed to pay an outstanding tax bill. But he refused to agree with speculation that Theresa Knorr had been planning a long trip somewhere. He believes to this day that she was being pressured for money by somebody. After speaking to the two detectives, Sullivan went over to the Salt Lake County Jail to try and see Theresa Knorr. Not only was he concerned about all that money he had loaned her, but he was also genuinely worried about her well-being. He still could not believe the murder allegations.

Bud Sullivan – who had never been near a jail before in his life – discovered the logistics of prison visiting are not as simple as one might imagine. Theresa's other good friend, Hal Cheney, had already been contacted by her and made a visit at noon that day. Prisoners were only allowed one visit per day.

Cheney – another clean-living character who had no previous experiences of the Salt Lake prison system – had got off to a bad start when he turned up at the jail's imposing entrance to be told there was no Theresa Cross in custody.

'But we have got a Theresa Knorr,' the prison warden informed him.

A few minutes later he walked into the stark visitors' room and watched through the glass partition as he waited for Theresa to appear. When she did walk out of a side door, Cheney was taken aback by seeing her in prison tunic and wearing little make-up. She looked very different from the charming, quietly confident lady he and his wife Fran had known for more than three years.

He hesitated, then picked up the phone to talk to his friend on the other side of the glass screen.

'I want you to know that I am innocent of the charges against me,' she told the pensioner before he had even uttered a word.

'I don't even know what the charges against you are,' replied a bemused Hal Cheney.

'I am charged with two counts of murder.'

For a moment there was silence. Cheney was visibly shocked by Theresa's admission. He tried to say something more to her, but it was so difficult to know what to talk about after that.

'Is there anything I can do for you?' he finally asked her.

'I could do with a toothbrush, some toothpaste. Those sort of things.'

Hal Cheney left Theresa a twenty-dollar bill and walked out of the visitors' room of the jail. He saw Theresa two more times, leaving a twenty-dollar bill at the end of each visit. But he later admitted – in an interview in February 1994 – that 'we never talked much. Just sort of sat and stared at each other.'

Theresa Cross called Hal Cheney from jail a few days later and told him, 'You don't really miss your freedom until you have lost it.'

Later in that first week of her detention, Theresa Knorr got a visit from her old friend at night school, Keith Bendixen. He arrived at the Salt Lake County Jail with a stack of religious books, only to be told he could not take any into the prison, in case he was hiding something in them to help her escape. Keith had an awkward fifteen-minute visit and has not seen Theresa since.

On 12 November, just before his departure back to California, John Fitzgerald visited the jail and asked Theresa Knorr if she would waive her extradition rights. She refused to and calmly told the investigator she had some things she wanted to take care of in Utah and had no intention of leaving if she could help it.

At Placer County Jail, on hearing of his mother's arrest, William Knorr met with task force member Chal DeCecco and insisted that his mother had admitted murdering her first husband and been involved in the death of her sister, Rosemary Norris, even though detectives had already discounted such suggestions.

NINETEEN

The most insidious effect of abuse is that it
dramatically increases the likelihood that the
victim-child will become a victim-spouse or
worse, a child abuser.

PAUL MONES, AUTHOR

At 10.00 a.m. on that same Veterans Day holiday, John Fitzgerald spoke to David Lundberg at the Sandy Police Department to see if he had come up with any record of Terry having told the police previously of her sisters' killings. Lundberg told Fitzgerald about all those domestic-violence calls from the house on Pepperwood where Terry lived with her in-laws, and how he had confronted one of his fellow officers in Sandy.

At 10.30 a.m. Fitzgerald contacted Terry at the house in Sandy and tried to get some more specific details on those earlier occasions when she told the police about what had happened inside the Knorr household. She mentioned telling a sheriff who came over to her friend Heidi

Sorenson's home, and she gave Fitzgerald the names of seven other people she had told over the years.

Fitzgerald was very concerned about these alleged earlier reports, and headed over to the Bountiful Police Department at 12.15 p.m. lunchtime to try and track down some concrete evidence of Terry's claims. All they could come up with was an address for Heidi Sorenson on West Center Road. Fitzgerald went straight over there, but no one was in, so he left his business card and a note asking her to contact him, and that it was urgent.

The following day, Fitzgerald went to the house in Bountiful where Theresa Knorr had worked before moving to Alice Sullivan's place. He was trying to fit as many pieces of the jigsaw together before he had to fly back to Sacramento.

Fitzgerald was fascinated by the way Theresa Knorr had changed her entire life after moving to Salt Lake City. Everywhere he went, people talked in glowing terms about her. It was as if she had reinvented herself.

It took Fitzgerald another three days of digging to uncover which cop Terry had spoken to when she met Heidi's friend the sheriff three years earlier. He located Woods Cross Police Department Chief Paul Howard and discovered that the report had been made by Clarence Montgomery. Fitzgerald then tracked down the name of the detective in Sacramento who handled the enquiry.

Meanwhile, Theresa Knorr continued to fight extradition back to California. That meant Smith and Fitzgerald would have to go back to Sacramento without their star defendant.

The *Sacramento Bee* – still following the investigation closely – ran a story on 13 November that rubbed disappointment into John Fitzgerald's wounds:

WOMAN CHALLENGING EXTRADITION IN DEATHS OF 2 DAUGHTERS Placer County sheriff's detectives returned empty-handed from Salt Lake City on Friday after learning that the woman charged with the murders of two daughters will challenge authorities' attempts to return her to California …

The following Monday, Theresa Jimmie Cross – charged in the torture slayings of two of her daughters – was formally arraigned when she appeared before the Third Circuit Court in Salt Lake City. She was ordered to be held without bail.

At the Placer County Jail, in California, William Knorr was scheduled to face a fitness hearing in the local juvenile court to decide whether he should be tried as an adult for his alleged crimes. He had been sixteen when Suesan was killed and seventeen at the time of Sheila's death.

Since the murderous antics of Ma Barker and her son Fred in the thirties, through the weird, sick killings by the creepy McCrarys, in Texas, to the sexually depraved California orgies of death committed by Gerald and Charlene Gallego, America has always loved families that commit heinous crimes. And now, in middle-aged Theresa Jimmie Knorr, it had the so-called ring leader in the flesh! Within days of the news of her arrest leaking out, Theresa Knorr's story and photograph became front-page news across the world.

First, high-profile coverage came in the prestigious *Los Angeles Times* on 14 November. In a lengthy front-page piece headlined UNBELIEVABLE TALE REVEALS GRISLY CRIMES, the paper reported all the details, peppered with quotes like, 'I have been here 33 years and I have never seen such a bizarre case' from Placer County Sheriff Donald J. Nunes.

Nationally syndicated talk-show host Sally Jessy Raphael requested interviews with the defendants and Terry. They were soon followed by *America's Most Wanted, Inside Edition.* Then came *USA Today*, the Associated Press and the *New York Times*, to name but a few.

In Placer County, Sheriff Don Nunes was juggling calls from CBS in New York and ABC in Washington. 'It is unbelievable, but it is understandable because of the savage behaviour involved. It's the motherhood aspect that has caused all this coast-to-coast interest,' the sheriff told one pressman.

Fierce competition between the news media – which the sheriff described as 'frothing at the mouth over this story' – had caused Nunes to back off and take a conservative approach. To avoid any facts from being misconstrued, Nunes insisted all news media queries were responded to with prepared statements.

'If Sally Jessy Raphael wants to come out here to talk, that's fine, but all legal questions will be referred to the district attorney,' he warned the ladies and gentlemen of the press.

Everyone, it seemed, wanted to talk to Terry Groves, the

one surviving daughter who had finally brought her mother's alleged crimes to the attention of authorities. KUTV's scoop in getting Terry in front of the cameras a few days earlier had undoubtedly been influenced by her own determination to remind authorities that, now that things were out in the open, she did not want her mother escaping justice. Now the whole world was requesting interviews with the brave daughter who had the courage to keep going back until someone listened.

Even the US tabloids – who usually ignore the most grisly crime stories in favour of celebrity tittle-tattle – got on the bandwagon. *Globe* headlines screamed, AMERICA'S MOST EVIL MOTHER. Accompanying the article was a photo of Theresa taken from her Utah driver's licence, complete with painted-on prison bars just to get the message over loud and clear to *Globe* readers.

Detective David Lundberg at the Sandy Police Department – who had bonded so well with Terry during the previous few weeks – found himself inundated with calls from journalists, screenwriters and Hollywood producers, all desperate for Terry's home phone number. He called her up and told her of all this interest, and she begged him not to tell any of them what her married last name was, let alone where she lived.

'I don't want to talk to anyone. You just screen all the calls for me,' pleaded Terry to her policeman friend.

So it was that Detective David Lundberg – eleven-year vet of the Sandy Police Department – became, in his own words,

Terry Groves's agent. It was an unusual move on the part of the young detective. Police officers do not often work as show-business representatives for witnesses in major murder investigations. But he explained, 'Terry wanted to get the story out, but she wanted it to go out in a proper way, without exploiting the death of her sisters. She also wanted to sell it for money. I was acting, and I hate to use this term, but I was acting, so to speak, like an agent for her.'

He soon found himself screening dozens of calls every day from aggressive Hollywood types, all desperate to sign up the rights to the Knorr story. Agent Lundberg dismissed all of them as being very untrustworthy, until Joe Dipasquale, of Quest Entertainment, came along.

'I had no experience, but I basically had to use my gut instinct, and I felt comfortable with this guy. He sounded very straightforward.'

On the Sunday morning before Thanksgiving, Terry Groves put on her one and only dress and escorted her husband Mike, her attorney and Detective David Lundberg to the Little America Motel, in downtown Salt Lake City, to meet Hollywood producer Joe Dipasquale. It was a controversial move on the part of both Terry and her policeman-turned-agent. Not surprisingly, the entire meeting was kept very quiet and not a word about it was ever revealed to the media at the time.

Dipasquale went over the contracts as the group sat in his suite. Terry asked a few questions about what writers the producer was planning to use and how the movie would be treated. Dipasquale reassured her it would be done very sensitively, and then she signed the contract.

A few minutes later the happy group were enjoying a slap-up brunch at one of the city's best restaurants. 'Let's celebrate with champagne,' announced Terry just before they started the meal. She ordered a bottle of Moet & Chandon and they made a toast. By signing that contract with Joe Dipasquale, Terry had just earned herself more money than she had in her entire working life – and it was all thanks to the alleged horrors inflicted inside the Knorr household. Agent David Lundberg also co-signed the same deal with the Hollywood producer. It is not known precisely how much he could earn from an eventual television movie of this extraordinary story which has not yet, to date, been made.

But officers with the Placer County task force are not so impressed. Inspector Johnnie Smith would only say of Lundberg's involvement, 'I don't know how legal it is.'

On 9 December, Theresa Knorr launched an all-out bid to prevent herself from ever being extradited to Placer County, California. She appeared before a Third Circuit Court commissioner, who stayed extradition proceedings after learning that her court-appointed lawyer had filed a petition seeking a writ of habeas corpus.

An indignant Theresa Cross – as she was now referred to – still insisted she was innocent of all the charges against her. She claimed she was not in California at the times of her daughters' deaths, and accused authorities in Utah and California of not having followed correct extradition procedures.

Theresa Cross's publicly appointed defender, Paul Quinlan, even conceded after the hearing that he was trying to buy time for his client – time to let the media hysteria in California and the rest of the world die down.

Quinlan knew full well that extradition warrants could only be attacked on limited fronts. Cross had three possible defences: she was not a fugitive because she was not in California when the crimes occurred; she was not the correct person being sought; or the court paperwork had a technical glitch.

County Prosecutor Bud Ellett said he expected to file a response to Theresa Cross's writ by the following week, and he warned that one of the Placer County task force investigators might be called to testify at the hearing. But court officials predicted at least a two-week delay on the extradition hearing. Despite this setback, Ellett assured newsmen at the court that he still believed she would be deported. It was just a question of time.

In Placer County, task force investigators tried to play down their disappointment by saying, 'Most of the evidence is pretty much intact. We've waited ten years. We can wait a little longer.'

In Auburn, California, William Knorr's attorney, Michael Brady – retained by DeLois Knorr for her husband – asked Placer County Judge J: Richard Couzens to delay his client's arraignment until 20 December. Brady said he wanted the extradition hearing in Utah to be completed first because he felt that William Knorr should be tried jointly with his mother. He also wanted to give attorneys time to research the question of the Knorr brothers being juveniles at the time of the alleged killings and how that would affect their eventual trial. Judge Couzens also appointed respected Auburn attorney Mark Berg to represent Robert Wallace Knorr, still in prison in Nevada for that unrelated murder. Berg told the court, 'My client may have been under sixteen at the time and there's some question about whether the district attorney can even prosecute them after all these years.'

Berg also insisted that the arrest warrant that was issued by the adult court might not be valid because of the age problem.

Luckily, Placer County investigator John Fitzgerald had a mole inside the Salt Lake City Police Department who kept him informed of every development as it occurred. Fitzgerald's pal, detective Marv Hammer, called him at Tahoe City to tell him the latest news.

'I've got a feeling that the judge is going to throw out her request at the next hearing,' Hammer told Fitzgerald. He promised his colleague in California that he would go to the hearing the next day and contact him as soon as he heard the judge's decision.

'Then you can come and get her before her attorneys file for any more delays,' promised Marv Hammer.

The following morning, Fitzgerald was pacing up and down his small office awaiting the all-important call. He had in his hand a written authorisation, personally signed by Pete Wilson, Governor of California, which empowered him to take fugitive from justice Theresa Knorr into his custody and then back to California. He also had a similar order from the Utah State Governor. The paperwork was all in, now he just needed his prisoner. Fitzgerald had even brought his packed overnight bag with him into work especially. At 10.30 a.m., Hammer came on the phone.

'You're on. The judge denied her request and she's free to go. The only stipulation is that you must bring a female officer with you.'

In Salt Lake City a devastated Theresa Cross had made a last desperate appeal to the judge by claiming that she could not fly because she suffered from sinus problems. The judge was not impressed. 'It won't hurt you' was his only response.

At the Tahoe City substation, Fitzgerald called Sheriff Don Nunes, who approved the trip to Salt Lake without hesitation and told his staff to book the investigator plus woman detective Laurie Ziegler on the next flight to Salt Lake City.

Fitzgerald and Ziegler checked into a motel in the centre of Salt Lake City, had a bite to eat and then called Marv Hammer to make arrangements to meet them at the Salt Lake County Jail at nine the next morning. Hammer made a call to the prison to ensure that the two detectives could get in without any last-minute problems over jurisdiction. Fitzgerald also insisted that Theresa Cross should not be told about the specific plans to extradite her until eight next morning – just in case she got her attorney to try more blocking tactics.

But Theresa Cross knew her departure for California was imminent. She just didn't know exactly when she would have to leave, so she put in a collect call to Alice Sullivan's son Bud and told him that she needed to hire another attorney to avoid extradition and ask if he could advance her $500.

'Theresa, I've advanced you everything I am going to,' came Bud Sullivan's terse reply.

Theresa Cross still insisted to Bud Sullivan that the $4600 he had loaned her the previous week had all been paid off towards her taxes. But Sullivan had been in touch with his bank and knew the cheque he gave Theresa had been cashed the day he loaned her the money. She must have been lying.

That last call to Bud Sullivan was the turning point for Theresa Cross. In her cell at the Salt Lake County Jail that evening, she meticulously drew a brightly coloured Christmas card for her close friends, Bud's sister Pat and her husband Vere.

The card consisted of three candles sparkling brightly with some holly below them on a piece of rough prison-issue paper. On the left side she had written, 'Merry Christmas and a Happy New Year.'

On the opposite side she wrote a message to her friends saying she was leaving for California and thanking them. 'Friends are as precious as fine gold,' wrote Theresa. She wished them a happy Christmas and signed off by saying, 'My thoughts are with all of you. Love Theresa.'

John Fitzgerald walked into Theresa Cross's prison cell at just before nine the next morning. She did not utter one word. Fitzgerald cuffed her unceremoniously with handcuffs that went around her waist and wrists and told her, 'There won't be any problems just as long as you don't cause me any problems. Our job is to transport you from Utah to California, and, if you just do as we ask, then it'll all be OK. You treat us decent, we'll treat you decent.'

Fitzgerald meant every word. Here was a classic opportunity to humiliate his notorious prisoner, but he preferred to allow her to keep some dignity.

At Salt Lake City Airport, Fitzgerald was relieved to see there was absolutely no sign of the expected media circus to greet them. Just before they got to the check-in area, he allowed her to hide her manacles under a small red coat. Then Fitzgerald, his prisoner – complete with that red coat, a floral blouse, and black pants – and Detective Ziegler found a quiet corner by the departure gate and waited for boarding to be announced.

After fifteen minutes Fitzgerald spotted, to his horror, a crowd of TV crews and reporters swarming up the corridor like a pack of hungry, noisy hyenas.

'There she is.'

'That must be her.'

They had been tipped off about that distinctive red coat. This time Theresa Cross was the one with no escape. She looked petrified. Even Fitzgerald felt a flush of anger. He just wanted to get his prisoner home to Auburn with the minimum of fuss and attention.

'We understand you are going to give us an interview,' one brazen reporter assured John Fitzgerald.

He was appalled that anyone should try to trick him so overtly. 'No way,' was about the politest Fitzgerald could be in the circumstances.

Just then the flight was called. Fitzgerald and Laurie Ziegler grabbed Theresa Cross by the arms and tried to march her through the waiting newshounds. Flashbulbs popped, but the crowd made way. One look at Fitzgerald's stern, determined expression told them not to push their luck.

Once on board, John Fitzgerald sat down with Theresa Cross between him and Ziegler. They made some pleasant, civilized small talk as the jetliner soared up out of the Salt Lake Valley and headed for California.

The conversation stayed mainly on an impersonal level. Theresa Knorr talked about Utah being a very nice place to live, that there were good people there and how the Mormons were very considerate.

But one particular comment by his prisoner stuck in John Fitzgerald's mind.

'People in Utah treat women much better than they do in California,' said Theresa Cross. She should know …

Fifteen minutes before landing at Sacramento Airport, Theresa Cross told her two police escorts she wanted to go to the bathroom. Fitzgerald undid her cuffs and escorted the sizable Cross as she waddled down the aisle towards the toilets. Before letting her in the cramped compartment, he checked it for any razor blades or other items that might have been left in there by previous occupants.

'OK. In you go, and don't forget to unlock the door the moment we knock on it,' explained Fitzgerald.

Theresa Cross squeezed into the toilet with just a tatty plastic bag containing her purse and a few items of make-up.

After four or five minutes, Fitzgerald and Ziegler looked at their watches anxiously and began to wonder why she had still not emerged. Fitzgerald calmly headed back down the aisle and knocked on the little door.

Theresa Cross emerged almost a completely different person from just a few minutes earlier. She was perfectly made up and had neatly brushed her hair. She looked almost glamorous, a bit like Roseanne Arnold's mother perhaps.

'There was a twisted vanity about her. Her appearance was always very important to her. She always tried to look good whatever the circumstances,' commented John Fitzgerald.

Theresa Cross had just spent five minutes ensuring that she would look her best when the plane landed and she found herself under the media spotlight. She wanted to be certain she would look as good if not better than everyone else. But it was all a delusion ...

TWENTY

'In ancient times, when might was right, the infant
had no rights until the right to live was ritually
bestowed. Until then the infant was a nonentity and
could be disposed of with as little compunction as
for an aborted foetus.'

SAMUEL RADBILL, AUTHOR OF *THE BATTERED CHILD*

Placer County Sheriff Donald J. Nunes is the kind of guy
who doesn't do things by halves. He also knows a good
press opportunity when he sees it, and the arrival at
Sacramento Airport of the by now notorious Theresa Knorr
on a Delta Airlines flight from Salt Lake City on 18 December
1993 promised to be a classic media event.

John Fitzgerald – sitting in his window seat as the plane
taxied to its terminal – was hoping, praying, that they could
get her down the steps and out of that airport with the
minimum of attention. As the plane came to a halt, he saw
Sheriff Nunes standing below him on the tarmac with the
reassuring sight of four Placer County officers. The sheriff
had even brought along his own dark blue Chrysler New

Yorker to whisk the threesome away as quickly as possible. Then Fitzgerald saw at least fifty members of the press, angling their cameras directly at the aircraft. There would be no easy escape.

As Fitzgerald, his prisoner and colleague Laurie Ziegler emerged at the top of the aircraft steps, the whirl of motor drives made Theresa Knorr's homecoming seem more like a presidential visit than the arrival of a woman alleged to be one of the most evil mothers of all time.

Once on the tarmac, Fitzgerald ignored the barrage of questioning and pushed Theresa Knorr and Ziegler in the backseat of the Chrysler before getting in front with the sheriff. Theresa Knorr looked terrified and said nothing.

But the press circus had only just got into gear. As the Chrysler screeched around the main terminal, journalists started chasing the car on foot. Every time the sheriff's car slowed down on the busy airport tarmac, a few healthy reporters caught up and tried to thrust their notebooks and microphones in the window. There was also another problem for the law officers – they could not leave the airport until they picked up Fitzgerald's Explorer, parked in the car park next to the main runway.

After circling around three more times and successfully wearing out even the fittest journalists, Sheriff Nunes pulled alongside Fitzgerald's car in the car park, and Ziegler, Fitzgerald and Theresa Knorr swapped vehicles hurriedly and headed off on the forty-minute drive to the Placer County Jailhouse at Auburn.

The brief Auburn winter, for which no one was ever quite prepared, arrived early the morning after Theresa Knorr's dramatic return to California. A bitter breeze flowed west from the Sierra Nevada Mountains and, in the great American tradition of public buildings in winter, it was so hot in the Placer County Courthouse, you felt trapped inside your clothes and there was nothing to breathe except thick steam heat.

First to be led into the immaculate, beige-coloured courtroom was Theresa Knorr, handcuffed and wearing ill-fitting regulation Placer County inmates' tunic and trousers in her favourite bright red.

The six television cameras, two still photographers, a radio reporter and two newspaper photographers allowed in the court recorded every move.

Theresa Knorr sat down opposite Judge J. Richard Couzens, the huge seal of the state of California between them. The stars and stripes were to the judge's right, the bear of the California state flag to his left.

No sooner had Theresa Knorr sat down on the brand-new maroon-coloured seat than her son William was brought in by two uniformed guards. They guided him alongside his mother. Neither looked the other in the eye. She kept her eyes set on the beige carpet. His eyes snapped around the room nervously.

William was terrified about sitting next to his mother. He had turned over a new leaf once he'd left his mother's home. Suddenly, that previous life had re-emerged and threatened his future. He looked pale and scared.

Then ex-husband Robert Knorr Sr. got up and screamed at Theresa Knorr. 'I hope you burn in hell for what you did to my kids, woman!'

The whole court stopped. Knorr Sr. glared. Reporters watched excitedly. Theresa Knorr glanced in the direction of her ex-husband and gave him a cool stare. It was a look that seemed to say: 'I am still in charge.'

Later Knorr Sr. claimed, as if to defend his actions, that he had reconciled with his son William and had been regularly visiting him in jail since his arrest. He said that his son was innocent and very depressed about the charges.

But his father's outburst in court that morning simply had the effect of making William Knorr look even more terrified. He leaned over and whispered a few words in the ear of his lawyer. Seconds later William Knorr was moved away from his mother to a row behind her.

In the public gallery, the assembled media watched in fascination because they knew that this was the first time mother and son had seen each other since those alleged crimes were committed inside that house just off Auburn Boulevard all those years earlier. Cameras continued to click. This was a photo opportunity none of them wanted to miss.

Theresa Knorr tried desperately to use her lawyer to shield herself from the family members and the press in the public gallery just ten feet away. She could feel the hatred emanating from her ex-husband, Robert Knorr Sr., DeLois Knorr, the daughter-in-law she had never met before, and a handful of friends who had come to court.

The press pack scribbled furiously. None of them was going to leave the steaming courtroom until every last detail of this first appearance of mother and son had been squeezed out.

A few minutes later the lawyer agreed to a continuance and the case was adjourned. Theresa and William Knorr were solemnly led away back to their cells. William Knorr's lawyer Michael Brady said afterwards that he hoped all future court appearances could be arranged so that mother and son were not in sight of each other. 'My client is distraught about being in court with her.'

Ironically, Brady also told newsmen after the court appearance that, although William Knorr wanted no part of being around his mother, he still felt it was best to keep the two defendants linked in court.

'If it is true that she was an overbearing mother, I want them tried together because she is responsible for the alleged homicide, not my client,' said Brady.

At the Placer County Jail attached to the courtroom, Theresa Knorr and her son William each occupied eight-by-ten cells in the part of the prison given over to solitary confinement for punitive or protective reasons. This was a high-profile case, and the protagonists of such dramas are often considered vulnerable to starstruck inmates happy to grab some glory by attacking notorious defendants.

Neither Theresa Knorr nor her son was particularly comfortable about their enforced incarceration, and –

although men and women inmates have been openly mixed inside Placer County's modern, air-conditioned facility since it opened in 1988 – they avoided each other like the plague. Weak, yellow-orange lights burned in both their cells most of the night, which was fine if you were an insomniac with plenty of books to read, but very distracting if you were not. The cells had a bed, a toilet, a sink, even a tiny desk balanced on lockers. In Theresa's, she had a three-inch window looking out on to a pond in a picturesque field at the back of the jail. Sometimes she watched pheasants hopping and skipping across the pastures as a few geese swam lazily back and forth in the pond. On another occasion, an orange-and-white-striped cat stalked a dove in the same field while a bluebird whistled in a small pine tree close by. On 22 January, Theresa Knorr was allowed a rare treat – a walk in the grounds. She also became a prolific letter writer and, from the day she arrived in Auburn, scribbled away furiously to all her friends back in Salt Lake City.

In his cell on the other side of the facility, William Knorr was allowed to work out in the weights room and then shower. The rest of the time he did push-ups and sit-ups. Both Knorrs were allowed to make collect telephone calls. But neither saw any newspapers or watched television. Jail rapidly started to become a way of life for them.

In Salt Lake City, many of those close friends of Theresa Cross, as she called herself in that city, were still reeling from the shock of her arrest and extradition to California.

Pat Thatcher, the daughter of Alice Sullivan, and her brother Bud Sullivan, had the unenviable task of boxing up all Theresa Cross's belongings and storing them away just in case she ever got back to collect them.

They carefully stacked her jewellery, make-up and books in cardboard boxes and then took all her clothes out of the cupboard in that porch area where Bud had built a rail to take all Theresa's extra clothing. They also dismantled a treadmill she had gone to great lengths to have delivered to the house, although it was rarely used by overweight Theresa.

Just as Pat was removing the last of Theresa Cross's dozens of pairs of one-inch-heeled pumps, she noticed a number of carefully wrapped gifts stacked neatly in the corner of the closet. The mother who allegedly had inflicted so much pain and suffering on her children had been looking forward to another friendly family Christmas in the Sullivan household and had already bought at least half a dozen gifts to give her new family.

'It was so sad. I took them down to the basement close to tears. I still cannot believe that a good person like Theresa could be responsible for the crimes she is accused of,' Pat said recently.

And Bud Sullivan continued to stoutly defend Theresa Cross, despite the fact she tried to trick him into lending her yet more money the night before her extradition to California.

'Maybe Theresa is protecting her kids and does not want to implicate the others and that's why she's saying nothing.

Maybe she was not involved in what they say. Who knows?'
Bud said.

TWENTY-ONE

'From victims in the home, they go on to become
victims and victimizers on the street.'

PAUL MONES, AUTHOR

Every day, investigators gathered at Inspector Johnnie
Smith's office inside the task force headquarters at
the Placer County Sheriff's Office in Auburn. On the walls
were maps of the region, as well as photos of Suesan and
Sheila, their mother and two brothers. Bagged-up evidence –
jewellery, clothing, make-up – still lay strewn on Smith's desk.

The detectives' job was prodigious. But the investigation
could have been even more complicated if Sheriff Nunes and
his officers had not taken full responsibility for both deaths,
despite the jurisdiction problems.

John Fitzgerald knew full well that Theresa Knorr's much
publicised arrest did not mark a slowing down of the
investigation process. On the contrary, he had to keep

pushing for nugget after nugget of information that would contribute to her eventual trial on murder charges alongside her two sons.

His main aim was to interview as many of the other Knorr family members and friends as possible. The task force was particularly interested in Knorr's oldest son, Howard Sanders. On 16 November, Investigators Smith and DeCecco reinterviewed him to clear up a few loose ends from his earlier statement on 3 November. They were especially interested in establishing exactly how Howard came to be informed of his sisters' fate. Sanders was fully co-operative, and no suggestion has ever been made that he was in any way involved in the deaths of his sisters.

Howard Sanders's wife Connie also provided a fascinating insight into life inside the Knorr household, including colourful references to black magic. She had also witnessed some of the abuse inflicted on the Knorr daughters.

Other important developments included the discovery of William Knorr's palm print on the popcorn-cup box that Sheila's crunched-up corpse was dumped in. Bonnie Paolini, latent print examiner at the California Department of Justice, must take credit for that and the later matching of two of William Knorr's fingerprints and one of his brother Robert's on a plastic bag found near the spot where Suesan died.

Meanwhile, brief court appearances at the Placer County Courthouse became Theresa and William Knorr's only glimpse of the outside world.

On the day I visited the court, Monday, 31 January 1994,

it was a crisp, sunny, fifty-degree winter day, with a cool wind cutting through from the mountains to the east. The first thing anyone inside the courtroom noticed was the fidgeting, grey-haired man sitting in the aisle behind me. He wore a shapeless suit and tie, not really in keeping with the man himself. His face was stern, steel-edged, but unemotional, almost devoid of expression. He looked dead ahead of him without blinking once. A slight belly bulged through his white shirt. That was Robert Wallace Knorr Sr., the father of four of Theresa's children.

And there was a sizeable cast of other characters there too.

DeLois Knorr, William's wife, glowered uneasily from the front row after acknowledging the presence of her father-in-law. William Hall, longtime friend and car-pool associate of William Knorr, looked on with concern. Another pal of William's was Nikolaas Bos. Both men later insisted their good friend was completely innocent of the charges. In the front row, a local TV newsman had set up his camera on a huge tripod, ready to get some fresh footage of mother and son the moment they appeared. At least a dozen other journalists, print and TV, filled the remaining rows of seats.

Just then, the expectant courtroom quietened down. Theresa Knorr, unemotional, her wrists cuffed at the front, was led into the hushed room from a door at the back of the court. Investigators told me before the court hearing that she had lost at least fifty pounds, thanks to the diet inside jail. Her face seemed sallow; the skin beneath her chin hung almost like a turkey's. The prison clothes, still her favourite crimson-red, did not help. Her hair was parted down the middle and frizzled from lack of conditioner. As cameras clicked in her direction, she seemed momentarily flustered. There was even a flicker of anger in her eyes. She was led to a chair at a table. She seemed relieved when her court-appointed lawyer, Mickey Sampson, appeared alongside her. From that moment on she played a game of cat and mouse with the waiting pressmen and family members by ensuring that Sampson blocked their view of her.

William Knorr, head bowed, was led in through the same wooden door as his mother had been a minute earlier. His wrists were cuffed at the front, his face pale in contrast to his bright, crisp and clean orange prison clothes. William walked to the middle row of seats well away from his mother and sat down, not looking up for even a second, in case he caught the eyes of the waiting family, friends, and media ... and worst of all, his mother, who sat just three feet in front of him.

Judge J. Richard Couzens referred to her as 'Miss Cross' throughout the brief hearing. Neither mother nor son was required to utter a word, but her lawyer, Sampson, made an interesting request to the judge. Centre stage at last, Mickey Sampson, in his mid-thirties, had a soft, dark beard, shaped so the round white baby jowls and soft chin didn't show. His longish, well-groomed, brown hair shining despite the onset of baldness, Sampson wore an inoffensive brown suit and had a friendly but somewhat anxious demeanour.

'We object strongly to her not being allowed to wear her

own clothes,' the public defender said. 'We ask that the order be lifted for her next court appearance so that Miss Cross be allowed to wear civilian clothes.'

The Honourable J. Richard Couzens denied the request and announced that 14 June 1994, would be the date of the case arraignment. Theresa Cross's vanity had outlasted two secret lives and the murder charges hanging over her head.

TWENTY-TWO

'And hope does not disappoint us, because God
has proved out his love into our hearts by the Holy
Spirit whom he has given us.'

ROMANS 5 (NEW TESTAMENT)

In her friendless cell at the Placer County Jail in Auburn, Theresa Cross was feeling lonely and confused, but still determined, no matter what, to keep in touch with friends from Salt Lake City.

On 12 January, 1994, Alice Sullivan's daughter got a moving letter from Theresa, which reduced her and her one-time tough cop husband to tears. She referred to 'how hard all this is on my friends. My lawyer said I will find out just who my real friends are.'

She insisted that, just because her children were saying things, they were not true. Theresa Knorr called her arrest and the charges 'a holocaust' and thanked her friends for standing by her in her 'darkest hours'. She even described her three-inch-wide cell window which overlooked a pond across the street and a little of the field below. She signed the letter: 'Love in Christ, Theresa.'

'It hardly seems the sort of letter a hardened criminal would write, does it?' Pat said after reading it. 'Whatever happens to Theresa, she will always have a friend in us.'

On the same day Theresa Cross's other good friends, Hal and Fran Cheney, got a letter from her that offers a true insight into her state of mind as she awaited trial. In it Theresa quoted Romans 5, from the New Testament: *'And hope does not disappoint us, because God has proved out his love into our hearts by the Holy Spirit whom he has given us.'* She said she read scriptures every day and had no one to talk to except the Lord our God.

Theresa Knorr also revealed that the jail chaplain had given her a new international version of the Bible and she had just finished reading the great lion of God, about Saul of Shish, which she found inspirational. She also read *Heaven and Earth*, about a Jew and a Catholic in the 1930s in Canada. She signed off 'In Christ Love, Theresa.'

Just two weeks later Theresa wrote another lengthy letter to Fran and Hal Cheney. Fran could hardly contain her emotion about her good friend Theresa and wept as she read this letter, written in blunt pencil. It referred to how twenty quails and six Canadian geese had flown over and decided to land on the pond outside her cell window. Seeing the geese made her realise how much she missed her freedom. She also came to appreciate the 'little things', like having tea and a piece of fresh fruit.

The Cheneys were so touched by the letter that they wrote back to Theresa promising they would come and see her at the Placer County Jail on their next trip to California. They also received a number of collect telephone calls from her after her extradition to California.

Meanwhile, at the Sullivan house where Theresa Cross was arrested on 10 November 1993, there was one lasting memory of the woman who devoted herself to looking after eighty-six-year-old Alice Sullivan. Still parked up in the driveway to the neat, suburban one-storey house remained Theresa's pride and joy, her 1986 Dodge, coloured her favourite crimson-red, naturally.

Theresa Jimmie Cross and her son William Robert Knorr remained in protective custody at the Placer County Jail in Auburn. Both mother and son were watched closely by corrections officers. In jail, Theresa continued writing vast numbers of letters, while William read books. He frequently made collect phone calls to his wife DeLois, and occasionally to his father, Robert Knorr Sr.

At the Nevada State Prison, in Ely, Robert Wallace Knorr initially refused to co-operate with investigators, and it was expected that he would be brought to Placer County to face the charges concerning his sisters' deaths before the next major hearing, in June 1994.

In Salt Lake City, Terry Knorr – her mother's only surviving daughter – found that the pressures of living under the same roof as her in-laws plus the worldwide publicity surrounding her allegations put an enormous strain on her marriage to Mike Groves. In February 1994 she reluctantly parted from her husband and moved back to the Sacramento area. Once again, mother and daughter found themselves living just a short distance apart, yet neither had any compulsion to meet.

The actual trial of Theresa Knorr and her two sons was scheduled for sometime in the early part of 1995. Meanwhile, Theresa Knorr met frequently with her lawyer, Mickey Sampson, as they tried to map out a defence strategy. He hoped to suppress any statements she made to investigators just after her arrest. The lawyer also intended to argue that, without a full videotaped confession or a written account of the alleged crimes, his client should not be held to statements made by individuals who might also be implicated in the killings.

An insanity plea was another option if Theresa fully confessed to the killings. But it would only be accepted after a rigorous fight. To be acquitted under such a plea, the defence had to prove that, at the time of each murder, the suspect was suffering from a mental illness or defect, and failed to know or appreciate that what she was doing was morally wrong.

Prosecutors were determined to ensure that Theresa Knorr and her two sons were found guilty and never went free. They pledged to fight an insanity defence by calling psychiatrists to testify that all three suspects knew precisely that what they were doing was wrong, and call into evidence the fact that the crimes were covered up after they were committed. They also intended to point out that Theresa Knorr and her sons methodically planned the murders and disposal of the bodies, and that they tried to conceal their connections to Sheila and Suesan by removing all evidence of actual identification.

But it was Theresa Knorr's only surviving daughter, Terry, who would play the most crucial role in the outcome of the case. Her key testimony about life inside the Knorr household and the deaths of her sisters was going to be vital to the prosecution case.

Meanwhile, Mark Berg, lawyer for Robert Knorr, was still insisting that Placer County had no business prosecuting the now notorious case because the family home was in Sacramento at the time of the killings.

'It is shocking that Placer County would attempt to prosecute a case where the victims and the defendants are from Sacramento,' Berg told reporters.

He intended to continue challenging the territorial jurisdiction issue because one of the homicides had no connection to Placer County. Berg insisted the jurisdiction issue was backed up by investigative evidence which showed Sheila Sanders died in the cupboard at the family apartment in Sacramento. He'd also noted that her body was found in an area fifteen feet inside the Nevada County side of the Placer–Nevada County line. Berg pointed out that state law allowed any county to prosecute as long as elements of the crime occurred in the prosecuting county. 'But there is no connection with Sheila's death to Placer County,' said Berg, insisting that either Nevada or Sacramento Counties – not Placer – had the right to prosecute. 'Whoever made the decision to burden Placer County taxpayers with this case acted irresponsibly,' added Berg.

Placer County District Attorney Paul K. Richardson was still reluctant to discuss the merits of the case. 'It would behove me to wait and see what [Berg] is going to file. We think we are on good ground to prosecute the case in Placer County,' he said.

Berg did concede that Placer County had jurisdiction to prosecute for the death of Suesan. But he also pointed out that Sacramento County had jurisdiction in Suesan's death as well because the defendants allegedly planned her death while at home in Sacramento. He continued to push for the two homicides to be dealt with together in one trial, in Sacramento.

DA Richardson admitted that his office had been in conversation with representatives of the Sacramento District Attorney's Office on the case, but he would not elaborate or confirm that Sacramento District Attorney Steve White had agreed to let Placer County handle both cases.

Robert Knorr's attorney Berg also believed Placer County Deputy District Attorney Dan Dong would try to justify doing the Sanders homicide in Auburn because the defendants had driven through Placer County while taking her body to its dumping spot in the Tahoe-Truckee area.

But, said Berg, transporting the dead girl's body through the county line did not justify having Placer County take over the prosecution. Berg warned that he intended to file the motion to challenge territorial jurisdiction as soon as his client, Robert Knorr, made an appearance in the Placer County Court.

* * *

As the legal system pressed ahead with its case against Theresa Knorr and her two sons, John Fitzgerald and the rest of the Knorr task force continued their investigations. They were still hunting for more clues to the killings, and continued to be stunned that with each breakthrough came yet more appalling details about life inside the Knorr household.

California's Department of Justice continued to examine the items found near both bodies in the hope that yet more evidence would be found, linking to the defendants. These included traces of blood, hair, fingerprints, even carpet fibres that might help confirm the awful events surrounding the killings of Sheila and Suesan.

A crucial part of Theresa Knorr's defence strategy was to be an extensive evaluation of her medical condition at the time she killed both her daughters. Forensic psychiatrists and psychologists had already begun to interview her at the Placer County Jail.

These 'mind experts' were called into every major homicide case soon after the arrest of a suspect. Their *modus operandi* was to initially interview the subject, having deliberately done the minimum of research on the case. Often nothing more than a newspaper clipping was read in advance of that first meeting because the mind experts prefered to hear a full account of a suspect's alleged crime in his or her words with their own interpretation of exactly what happened. That alone helped the psychiatrist or psychologist during initial evaluation of a crime.

After that first interview with Theresa Knorr was concluded, the mind experts began a painstaking research process that included collecting information from a vast range of sources including relatives, medical notes, school reports, comments from employers and witness statements for both defence and prosecution. Even notes that police collected about her general background were deemed useful.

These psychologists wanted to delve into Theresa's family history before she met and fell in love with her first husband. They even probed her own childhood for evidence of incidents that might help to explain her later actions as a mother. It was highly likely that she herself was either molested or sexually abused as a child. Her parents' attitudes towards crucial elements of her upbringing, like sex, money and love, would also have shaped her later domestic problems. Undoubtedly, the premature death of Theresa Knorr's mother was considered as a significant turning point in her childhood. Opening up her mind could be the key to understanding why Theresa Knorr committed such horrendous crimes against her own flesh and blood.

TWENTY-THREE

'The violent act becomes necessary as a means
of asserting the will and compensating for real
or imagined humiliation.'

BRIAN MASTERS, AUTHOR

The Knorr case presented an extraordinary opportunity for
riminal experts to examine in minute detail the background and circumstances of a series of killings that was unique
in its very nature because of the close family ties between the
victims and their killers.

In the eyes of many, Theresa Knorr and her two sons
qualified as serial killers if found guilty of the charges they
faced in the deaths of Suesan and Sheila. The term 'serial
killer' usually referred to criminals who did not kill their
victims simultaneously. In other words, there was a period of
time between each death.

This was not to be confused with the description
'repeater', used when referring to criminals jailed following

the killing of one victim and then released from prison only to murder again.

Criminologists across the globe were watching the Knorr case closely. British forensic psychiatrist Dr Peter Wood was particularly intrigued by the case. 'It is extraordinary in itself that she [Knorr] killed her own flesh and blood. But to apparently be a joint serial killer with her two sons is even more unusual.'

Dr Wood had investigated the minds of many killers over the years and gained a unique insight into their behaviour. But even he was astonished by the circumstances behind the deaths of Suesan and Sheila.

After some careful consideration of the facts behind the case, Dr Wood concluded, 'The mother who kills her children when they are older is likely to be either schizophrenic or paranoid psychotic.'

Dr Wood believed that the most significant allegation concerning the crimes that Theresa Knorr had committed was that she apparently managed to kill twice – and on separate occasions – as well as using the help of two of her own sons.

Dr Wood explained at the time, 'That makes her less likely to be psychotic because she has involved others. If you are driven by delusion, unless you draw someone else into your own delusions, the motive for killing is foreign to the person you are trying to involve in your behaviour. Almost by definition, people who kill jointly are not psychotic. That's the simplest way of putting it.'

Dr Wood has dealt with a number of cases that contained relevant aspects to the case of Theresa Knorr and her two sons. One of his patients killed her ten- and twelve-year-old daughters together in cold blood in the north of England some years ago. The woman was diagnosed as depressed, and she'd been treated for depression before her feelings of resentment towards her daughters manifested themselves into the tragic killings.

Initially, she tried to feed her daughters a lethal cocktail of drugs and alcohol to snuff out their young lives. But, when that failed, she bludgeoned and stabbed them to death in the front room of their family's tiny terraced home after she had sent her unsuspecting husband out to get a birthday cake for one of the little girl's birthdays.

The woman was proclaimed a paranoid schizophrenic. Afterwards she admitted to Dr Wood that she would have killed her husband if she could have found him – a significant statement when one considers the obvious hatred that existed between Theresa Knorr and Robert Knorr Sr.

There are also indications that Theresa Knorr was suffering from delusions at the time she and her children were living together in Sacramento. Some of the incidents recalled, in police statements, by her relatives and friends reveal overt paranoia.

But the woman killer treated by Dr Wood differed from Knorr in one crucial way. She was deeply depressed by the awful deaths she inflicted on her daughters, and attempted suicide shortly after their deaths. There is no evidence that

Theresa Knorr felt any guilt about killing her own flesh and blood.

However, just like Theresa Knorr, this woman was completely wrapped up in her own feelings and thoughts. Knorr's self-imposed seclusion inside the family's house for weeks on end appeared to be clear evidence of her inverted state at the time.

Dr Wood spent many months gently coaxing his patient to confess her true motives for ending the lives of her own children. The forensic experts lining up to interview Theresa Knorr were already finding similar problems in extracting information about her true feelings. Knorr's life in Salt Lake City following the deaths of her daughters clearly indicated that she'd neatly compartmentalised the killings so that they would not remain constantly on her conscience. In other words, she was in a complete state of denial about the horrendous crimes she allegedly committed.

Another interesting parallel between Dr Wood's case and the Knorr killings was that the psychiatrist's patient became – just as Theresa Knorr apparently did – completely paranoid about her neighbours. She felt that people in the street were constantly spying on her, running her down and criticising her for the way she looked after her children.

Following the departure of Robert Knorr Sr., Theresa Knorr's loving care and attention for her children completely broke down. It was as if she had developed an overwhelming sense of responsibility for all the family, and her way of getting out of that was to abuse those people she was responsible for. Theresa Knorr and her two sons.

One of the most astonishing aspects of the case – regardless of the eventual legal outcome – was that it took so many years for Theresa Knorr and her sons to be brought to justice. Terry Knorr's efforts to alert authorities to the killings have already been well documented in this book, but there was another aspect that has so far been overlooked – the inability of the police to come up with any profile of the murderer of the two girls, even though it was clear they had both been unlawfully killed (although authorities had not linked the deaths at that time).

Many criminologists believed that too much emphasis was being put on profiling killers. Often, some insisted, these profiles proved wholly – or certainly partially – inaccurate. In the cases of both Sheila and Suesan, no actual profiles were produced because investigators believed they did not have enough clues to build up a picture of the girls' killers. They were also unaware of the family connection.

Privately, police in Placer County admitted that was the precise reason why so little action was taken initially to track down the killers. In fact, over the past two decades, investigators had become so used to using profiles to help bring killers to justice that, when no such 'picture' existed, many police inquiries simply fizzled out.

Since the deaths of Suesan and Sheila all those years previously, police homicide units had become far more sophisticated in their investigations and tracking of killers. Detectives tended to be strictly reactive up until the late 1980s. When a murder was reported, investigators gathered what evidence they could, traced the victim's identity and tried to reconstruct the crime from what they could determine about the victim's movements during his or her final hours. If there were witnesses, they were interviewed also. But this procedure failed miserably when dealing with episodic, apparently motiveless killings. The reason for this was simple: such crimes did not fit into any set pattern. The motive for murder is not dependent upon the particular situation or upon the individual victim. In this case, without an identity or any clues as to the allegedly domestic nature of the girls' deaths, police were left with next to nothing.

The truth of the matter is that reactive homicide investigations depended upon things like weight of evidence, clues at the crime scene, relationship between victim and the murderer, involved witnesses or passers-by, and, finally, the fear and guilt of the killer him or herself. In the case of Suesan and Sheila, the police were virtually empty-handed.

Chillingly, in the previous ten years more than twenty-five per cent of all murders in the United States had been 'stranger' homicides in which the killer was not driven by any apparent rational motive and, since detectives looking into the deaths of the two girls did not even have their identities, they could not link the killings with anyone. Investigators naturally found such cases frustrating because the killer might be in the area for only a short time before disappearing. Worse still, in rural areas like the Sierra Nevada Mountains, there were the added problems of jurisdictions that do not routinely share information about unsolved homicides. The alleged killers of Suesan and Sheila were never even the target of a combined task force, until after Terry Knorr had finally persuaded investigators to act upon her claims.

At the time of both girls' deaths, detectives only had a crime scene as evidence. They had absolutely nothing else to go on until after the autopsies, and even those medical examinations did not provide many additional clues other than incidentals which proved fruitless to investigators. They also faced further investigative problems because both girls died – or were near to death – in a different location from where they were eventually dumped. This created, in effect, two crime scenes, and caused added confusion to the detectives until they began a piece-by-piece search of the homes where the girls had lived. But again, this was *after* Terry's story had finally been believed. Interestingly, many experts believe that the killer who strikes first and then takes the bodies to a remote location is less in control.

Another factor that undoubtedly helped the killers of Suesan and Sheila avoid detection for so long was the lack of publicity the girls' deaths attracted. Front-page news in local newspapers was hardly enough to raise any real interest outside of the immediate communities where their corpses were discovered. In retrospect, the lack of any real press and TV coverage for those killings helped keep the police efforts out of the spotlight, and, arguably, if the case had received more publicity, then someone further afield might have recognized the descriptions of the bodies and done something about it. Further, it should be pointed out that, although family members recall seeing small mentions of the killings at the time, more extensive coverage might have prompted them to react more positively.

Detectives have also speculated that the killers of the two girls found it easy to put the murders to the back of their minds because there were so few reminders of their crimes in the newspaper and on the television. What is important about the profile of a killer from a police officer's point of view is that it's impossible to see a complete picture of the criminal's motivation until well after he or she has been apprehended and diagnosed. Police training still focused on the traditional murderer who was not compelled to murder and who fled because he feared the police and prosecution. Often the episodic killer will go on committing enough crimes to ensure his own destruction. What made the killers of Suesan and Sheila so difficult to apprehend was that they stopped killing.

One senior homicide detective summed it up by saying, 'The breaks usually only come by chance.' Another crucial aspect of the initial police investigation was whether the killer or killers were confident enough to spend time at the crime scene, or whether they felt the need to leave it immediately after killing and/or dumping the body. Again, the evidence to police in the Sierras was minimal. Any normal investigation never stood a chance.

TWENTY-FOUR

'Everyone has the capacity to kill.'
FORENSIC PSYCHIATRIST PETER WOOD

Initially, Placer County Superior Judge J. Richard Couzens ruled out any attempts to move the eventual murder trial to Sacramento and lawyers' demands that William Knorr be tried as a juvenile. He was now 26 and, if found guilty, would have to serve his time in an adult correctional facility.

However, Judge Couzens did grant William bail after hearing that he was considered a 'minimal flight risk'. Five friends and associates testified that he was a young man of exemplary character and led a stable homelife. The prosecution demanded $1 million bail but the judge eventually set William Knorr free once he'd posted $150,000.

Meanwhile, brother Robert remained in Nevada State Prison after his lawyer Mark Berg held off his extradition.

Detective Fitzgerald eventually brought William back to California to stand trial on 29 June 1994.

Then, following a jurisdictional debate between Nevada and Placer Counties, it was concluded that, unless the case was moved to Sacramento, there would have to be two separate trials. On 12 August 1994, Judge Couzens ordered the trial of Theresa and her two sons to be moved to Sacramento County.

Away from the court battles, Theresa's fragmented family were trying with great difficulty to get on with their lives. Former husband Bob Knorr located Suesan's unmarked grave in the Auburn County Cemetery and purchased a small headstone for his daughter. Meanwhile, Howard Sanders had become engaged to be married and had started training to be a chef.

Less than a year after William's arrest, his wife DeLois left him, although he continued to remain close to Bob Knorr and his family, as well as numerous friends and associates. Out on bail, William got himself a job and counted the days until he was due in court.

At Sacramento County Jail, newly arrived Robert was living in the protective-custody unit where he read and wrote while hoping that one day the nightmare orchestrated by his mother might be over. Robert intended to enrol for a college degree course in psychological counselling once he was returned to Nevada State Prison to complete his other murder sentence.

Then, in late 1994, Robert volunteered to provide prosecutors with complete testimony in exchange for reduced charges. A week before Christmas, the DA dropped all the charges against him which involved Suesan's murder. The only charge still standing was a single count of conspiracy to aid his mother in the murder of Sheila.

At most of Theresa's court appearances during this period she remained quiet and composed, although many later recalled that her face seemed to be in an almost permanent scowl. Only once, in November 1994, did she lose her temper and eventually faint.

In early 1995, Theresa accepted that her lawyer should seek a sanity hearing to decide whether she was fit enough to face trial. She shaved her head and underwent more examination by two psychiatrists who both completely disagreed on her mental state of health. One said she was deeply deluded and unable to come to terms with what she had done while another insisted she was perfectly fit and well. One local reporter then revealed Theresa treated jail as 'just a hotel with really bad room service'. A formal sanity hearing was eventually set for June 1995.

Meanwhile, the only surviving daughter Terry continued to find it difficult to have a 'normal life'. She'd already divorced and remarried and filed for divorce again. Then Terry headed off for California from Utah and briefly held down jobs as a babysitter, manicurist, fast-food waitress and maid. Terry was paying $50 a month to sleep alone in a lean-to next to a mobile home on a trailer park in southwest Sacramento.

Terry then tried a reunion with her most recent husband, Bill Gilbert, but it ended with another split-up two months later. Terry suffered her second tubal pregnancy in April 1995, and doctors confirmed that she would never be able to have children after those beatings at the hands of her mother. After recovering from that shocking news, Terry told friends she wanted to raise enough money to open a home for abused children.

Theresa, thin and gaunt, looked defiantly over at Sacramento courtroom judge William R. Ridgeway as the case against her finally opened on 17October 1995. Since she had lost all that weight, her baggy clothes and sagging skin seemed in marked contrast to the once grossly obese parent from hell.

The court heard of the horror of Theresa's appalling crimes including the murders and the abuse she'd thrown at her children over a long period of time.

Prosecutor John O'Mara told the court, 'While she's down at Chowchilla [women's prison] getting three hots and a cot, her children will be having all the nightmares and bad dreams that go with all the things she said and did to them. She's saddled them with so much emotional baggage they are never going to come out of this whole.'

Yet more psychologists' reports presented to the court diagnosed Theresa as suffering from multiple personality disorder while other so-called mind experts insisted she had a genuine grasp of reality and definitely understood the difference between right and wrong. They also labelled her as narcissistic — completely self-obsessed.

Theresa's lawyer Hamilton Hintz insisted to the court that she was a victim of an abusive home life as a child and young wife. Hintz said his client 'never had a fair chance in life'. He also told the court about Theresa's four marriages, six children and how she struggled to keep the family afloat. 'She was raising these kids as best she could when she was still a child herself,' added Hintz.

But presiding judge Ridgeway later described the allegations against Theresa as 'callousness beyond belief' in his summing up. Rideway had also been particularly moved by a letter from Robert Knorr Jr. 'She cruelly and calculatingly tortured her victims both physically and mentally over the course of years, killing them in every way possible, over and over again,' wrote Robert.

Robert also insisted in his letter that his mother had destroyed her family, either through murder, torment or abandonment. 'We have all been sentenced to life without parole, reliving our own private nightmares in the early hours, imprisoned in our memories.'

Eventually, Theresa gave evidence after being instructed by her Lawyer Hamilton Hintz to stand. With a faltering voice, she pleaded guilty to charges of murdering her two teenage daughters Suesan and Sheila. When the judge asked her if she accepted her own guilt and appreciated her responsibility for her crimes she muttered, 'Yes.'

As part of a pre-agreed arrangement, the prosecutors did

not demand the death penalty because of her guilty pleas. Theresa, then 49, was given two consecutive life sentences and told that she would not be eligible for parole until she was 81 years of age.

Robert Knorr was sentenced to three years in a state prison and the court ordered the sentence run concurrently with his 1991 murder sentence. At thirty-five years old, he'd spent almost a third of his life in prison. In 1998, Robert made the honour roll of a Lovelock high school that offered courses to inmates. He earned a diploma in 1999 before enrolling as a psychology major at a community college near his prison. Robert became eligible for parole in 2001 and is now believed to be working as a counsellor to problem juveniles in northern California.

William Knorr was given probation for the part he played in the murder of his sisters and was ordered by the court to undergo therapy. William is now divorced and lives and works in a Sacramento suburb.

The oldest surviving child, Howard Sanders, moved to Michigan and his half-sister Terry believes he has married again and had more children.

But it's Terry who has clearly suffered the most. Since the end of her mother's trial, she has swapped homes and partners on a regular basis. A drink-driving arrest led to her being committed to a Kansas women's self-help home for six months. She's also regularly been involved in bar-room brawls which have led to spells in hospital.

Terry's courage in helping bring her mother to justice has

led to numerous appearances on TV talk shows. During many interviews, she reiterates her dream to open a children's home in the name of her two murdered sisters. But, for the moment, Terry continues to fight those demons, which have never truly allowed her to develop as a 'normal' person.

By the end of the 1990s, Terry was out of contact with her brothers William and Howard and only heard from Robert occasionally. She'd also gained a lot of weight and lived in fear of turning into another version of her mother.